The Super Supervisor

D1506598

Table of Contents

Acknowledgements

Most of the phraseology in this book has come from my association with working people for more than four decades. It is the language of the employee. When a phrase, rhyme, or catchword has been used to present an idea, I have given credit to the source where I was aware of it. Reference to any material I did not originate, whether it was from a preacher, supervisor, TV program, or lecturer, is not meant to imply that I take credit for it.

I gladly acknowledge all the assistance I had from those who share my desire to help others in dealing with the problems of living and working.

This book is respectfully dedicated to Mr. Jack Greer, without whose confidence and encouragement it would not have been written.

The Super Supervisor

An employee speaks out on the sins of management and the overlooked secrets of motivation in the work place.

Things your employees always wanted to tell you, but were afraid you would fire them.

This book is based on texts of a presentation I have had the opportunity to make to thousands of management teams around the country since 1981. I am delighted to present it now in book form for those who may be interested in the views of a non-expert on human relations, with emphasis on the labor/management relationship.

Mildred Ramsey

An Employee's View

The Super Supervisor is an employee's view of the labor/management relationship. I spent more than 40 years as an hourly paid production worker in a labor-intensive industry —textiles, in several different jobs for several different companies.

It always has been my firm conviction that enlightened management is all a worker needs to promote his productivity and assure his future in the work place. Sticking to this conviction in good times and bad, in times of discontent and union movements, has brought me a certain amount of attention, not all of it favorable. It also got me a lot of speaking engagements.

The experiences of more than four decades on the job, observing the labor/management relationship, and my work as a pro-freedom activist have developed in my mind some very firm philosophies of how the supervisor and the supervised can work together best to achieve mutually desired goals. Many management people who have heard me speak from my shop floor experience have suggested that some of my thoughts, ideas and observations be put into print. This book attempts to do that, with the hope that every level of management will find at least a few points to use in daily relationships with the greatest resources any business has—interested, inspired and productive employees.

I sometimes tell my audiences that listening to me is something like panning for gold. You have seen old prospectors on TV up in the mountains dishing up gravel in big pans with holes in the bottoms, shaking, washing and shaking some more before throwing out the gravel. If they are lucky, they find a tiny nugget among the sand and unusable debris. After you have thrown out all the gravel in this book, I hope you will find at least one little nugget that will enrich your personal relationships with people in your world; especially in the delicate, intricate, all-important relationship between the supervisor and the supervised.

I got one idea for this book when I heard a labor consultant compare the labor/management relationship to a person training a dolphin. He said that when the trainer wanted the dolphin to jump through a hoop, he would stand in front of it holding out the hoop in one hand, extending a fish in the other. Waving the fish he would command the dolphin to "jump."

Of course, the speaker was talking about rewarding employees after they "jump." That was his view, but I felt that these trainers need to hear the dolphin's viewpoint; so, I'm the dolphin and I'm going to tell you what makes me jump—and it ain't fish!

I am not trying to imply that I know anything about managing. If I could manage, I would not have stayed on a production line 42 years, would I?

I feel sort of like the man who said he did not know music. He said a sheet of music looked like a bunch of little black balls climbing a fence. But, while he didn't know music, he could tell the moment someone got out of tune or off key. So it is with employees. We do not know management, but we know when you are out of tune or off key.

I am going to tell you some areas where you may be off key and out of tune in the eyes of your subordinates. You have heard it from labor lawyers, labor consultants, labor advisors and labor leaders.

Now hear it from labor.

The value of the sensitive, positive approach in interpersonal relationships is universal. It will work on your spouse, your children, parents, relatives, neighbors, students, friends —even your enemies. So, although most of this book is addressed to labor/management relationships, I hope all who read it will find something to enrich their relationships with all the people in their world. You will get a favorable response from almost anyone if you try a little "positive communication."

It is simple, sound, cost-free—and it works!

3

The Mixed Up Priorities
Of Management

Over the years, management has renovated, remodeled, restructured, reorganized, revitalized and revolutionized every aspect of its operations except one—its relationship with employees.

While corporations and organizations large and small have adopted the most advanced discoveries in technology, utilized the latest in architectural design, and spent untold millions on management training programs, the astounding truth is that the vast majority of management teams still do not know what makes their employees "tick." As a result, they are not getting top job performance from their workers on a continuing basis.

Contrary to the prevalent idea among the general public and to the theme song of labor unions, "overwork and under-pay" is not the cause of long-standing discontent among working people that keeps them from giving their best efforts to their employers.

As an employee, I believe the problem is a negative and insensitive system of management that dehumanizes the worker and often puts him in the same category as the machinery and other fixtures in far too many work places. We are hearing a lot these days about "humanizing management techniques" and I believe this is an idea whose time has come. In my opinion, it is long overdue because the basic undercurrent of dissatisfaction that dominated the thinking of employees in 1942 when I entered the work force is still there today.

It is a reaction to insensitive management that says "Management doesn't care about me; all the boss cares about is the job or what he can get out of me."

I could not begin to estimate the number of times I have heard an employee say—and have said myself—"all I want from management is to be treated like a human being."

Exactly what does an employee mean when he makes this kind of statement?

We will be analyzing this and other feelings of employees throughout this book and I hope all who read it will get a better understanding of working people and that better relations between the worker and the boss will result.

As far as I know, this is the first in-depth study of an employee's perspective regarding the labor-management relationship and it should be noted that nothing I write or say is meant to reflect unfavorably upon any company I have worked for, and certainly not the wonderful company where I wound up my working years.

Human Kindness—A Motivator

My prayer and heart's desire is that these opinions will give a basis for a greater appreciation of the labor/management relationship and a new motivation to improve whatever conditions exist in each individual work place.

Mr. Supervisor, you must take the initiative here and if some workers are slow to respond you must hang in there with a program of sensitive and humane management techniques until they do respond. Treat your people right. Use a positive approach and employees will repay you with performance.

Another thing to keep in mind is that I do not think every one of my ideas will work every time in every work place. I am an hourly paid employee and all my points are made from the production worker's perspective, with the hope that everyone will get at least one idea that will help the boss and worker understand each other better.

As I said, I am not trying to tell you how to manage, but how your employees wish you would manage.

If I sound critical and accusing at times, it is because I have such strong feelings on this subject. (A lot of employees do, but haven't had the opportunity to speak out.) I appreciate the hard work and expertise of the management team, whose dedication and attention to detail affects us all on the job every day. However, you forget sometimes that nothing on your agenda for any day is more important than developing a continuing positive pact of mutual respect, trust and affection with your workers.

Your employees are not personnel—they are PEOPLE.

My main purpose is to remind you, again and again, that your people are more than hands and a back. They have minds and, more importantly, they have hearts. If anyone in your world is angry at you, it probably is not because you have hurt them physically or mentally, but because you have hurt them emotionally—you have wounded their feelings or spirits.

When employees say "a human being," they are talking about the FEELING human, not the thinking one or the acting one. If your subordinates, or anyone you know, are bitter toward you and you are not getting satisfaction out of your relationship, it is because they have been hurt emotionally and have slammed their heart's door on you. You never will have a good relationship with these people until you relate to them in the emotional realm.

Every person in your world has feelings or emotions; some wear them on their sleeves, others keep them deep inside, but they all will respond to the same stimuli—kindness, consideration, courtesy and compassion.

Mr. Supervisor, you have to put some "heart" into your management techniques if you want your people's best efforts on a continuing basis. You must bring the touch of human kindness back into the work place.

If you are in management, look for the various dimensions of your employees and try to understand what makes them "tick." This will enable you to relate to them in a more caring, positive and sensitive manner and I guarantee they eventually will respond. The result will be a more productive-minded, quality-conscious and company-loyal work force which will be steadfast in support of you and your mutual goals.

It is something worth looking into, Mr. Employer. There is something in it for you besides contented, productive employees. This is the kind of "stuff" that prosperous and secure businesses are made of.

Use this book and all the ideas you can get to help you renovate, remodel, restructure, reorganize, revitalize, and maybe even revolutionize, your employee relations through what I call "super supervising."

The 'Gap' Between
Labor And Management

During my 42 years in the work place, I have found a common thread that binds most working people together—we all want to be treated "right" by our supervisors on the job. Evidently there are a lot of employees out there who feel they are not getting this kind of treatment from management. A recent survey revealed that 85 percent of American workers are not satisfied with their jobs. This figure may surprise some, but, from my own experience and from complaints I have heard from others, I have to believe that a cold, critical and uncaring method of management is a fact of life in most industries and organizations in this country today and always has been. Starting at the top level, it is passed down, with every superior browbeating his subordinates until it comes down to the employee who has no one to pass it on to.

How management can be so far advanced in some areas and so far behind in this one most important aspect of its operation is something employees have wondered about since the industrial revolution began. It should be said to management's credit that the unique morale problem and employee negativism we see today is not all management's fault. However, in my years "in the catbird seat" observing labor/management relations, I don't think I ever have seen employee discontent more widespread or morale so low as it is today.

I believe the reason for a lot of the unrest particular to this decade is nobody's fault. Because of recession, excessive government regulations, foreign imports, high interest rates, unprecedented demands by labor unions, changing employee behavioral patterns, etc., thousands of industries and management teams are "against the wall." Some are in great upheaval and confusion, fighting for survival. Many are doing their very best for their employees and finding it is not enough.

Why? Because of the "gap" between management and labor and the secretive, evasive efforts of management to keep employees in the dark about the operation. Most employees do not understand fully what is happening in the business world today and how it relates to them.

The economy had been booming for so long that we all took it for granted. Everybody was riding high and for years there was a time of "anything goes" in the work place—or almost anything. Markets were wide open, buyers were taking anything that came down the pike, regardless of quality of workmanship. It seemed like the best of worlds for the worker because during this economic "high" management gradually lightened the work loads and hired large numbers of un-needed people. Companies loosened rules of discipline and gross misbehavior often was tolerated on the job. Management let up on its push for excellence of performance in stressing volume and few employees felt inclined to give their best efforts.

Both management and labor lost the urgency to produce quality products and services for their customers—the worst of all scenarios for any business.

Then the axe fell. The boom burst. Recession was the word.

No longer would buyers accept inferior merchandise. They found they could get better quality products from overseas and billions of dollars and thousands of American jobs left the country. Corporate complacency vanished. Markets tightened, even for highest quality goods and services and competition became even more fierce.

In order to survive, employers had to make drastic and desperate changes. Management teams were ordered to tighten up, take back and bear down—and workers had to go back to work.

Boom-time surplus employees had to go, work loads were increased and job performance became a condition of employment, not an option. Many employees today view this "about face" by employers as mistreatment and meanness on the part of management because they never have been educated about the connection of their organization to the rise and fall of the economy and to market conditions and fluctuations.

There will be a chapter later about the importance of employee education, and some suggestions on company-sponsored courses—and I hope you are reading carefully, Mr. Manager.

I believe employee training classes will be the wave of the future, because the more informed workers are, the more they will understand labor/management objectives and the harder they will work. Education precedes dedication.

Mr. Manager, the answer to your problems is under your nose. Take your case to your people. Take employees into your confidence. Renovate and remodel your employee relations. Oh, I know some good steps have been taken and management teams all over the world are TALKING about updating their labor/management relationship. You hear a lot about "industrial democracy," "human resource development" and "quality circles" and all this is great, but from my contacts with working people and the morale problem we have today, I am afraid most management teams are preaching something they are not practicing in the work place.

Their programs are sensible and sound, but they have not been moved from the drawing board to the shop floor.

In various meetings and publications, management talks about "caring" for the employee and how important employees are to the success of the operation, but, in most instances, nobody makes the employee FEEL like an important participant who is making a specific contribution to that success.

Making this happen is what this book is all about.

You see, it is one thing to read in a paid-for local newspaper ad that the Wacky Widget Company "appreciates" its employees, but an entirely different thing to have a Wacky Widget first-line supervisor walk up to an employee and say something like this (and free, too):

"Jim, you broke new ground last week when you solved that problem with the Widget molder. Not only will it help us in this department, but the ripple effect will benefit the entire company. I appreciate you and your interest in your job."

Mr. Manager, you need "human resource development" on the shop floor, not in the file cabinet in the office. You need "employee relations improvement" in the work place, not the conference room. You need "individual employee recognition" on the job, not just in seminar classes.

Stop preaching and start practicing.

Stop talking the best game in town and start playing it. Stop trying to impress the world with your benevolence and fairness. Impress your employees and the world will hear about it.

Working With 'Change'

I have been studying recent "changing employee behavior patterns" as one reason for loss of worker support and loyalty. An encounter with a psychiatrist got me interested in this concept:

In recent years, millions of words have been written and spoken about the changing behavioral patterns of employees and the need for management to address this critical aspect of its operation by changing the way it manages. You must change the way you manage because the people you manage have changed.

All the experts agree that the old way is out. They say that people who are filling up the work force today have a different value system than those who are leaving and retiring. They tell us there is a scientific reason for this.

Psychiatrists say that a person's value system is locked in when he is around 10 years old. It is not what he HAD when he was 10, but what he DID NOT HAVE that shaped his priorities more or less for life. What the older employees, those retiring and leaving the work force now, didn't have at age 10 was money or financial security. (There had been a depression.) Financial security is tops in their list of priorities. As long as you pay well, you can manage them any way you please. But, younger workers had money when they were 10. Mama had gone out and got a job.

Financial security is not number one with them. What they didn't have at 10 was EMOTIONAL security. They had a key to get in the house; Mama and Daddy were both working and "doing their thing." Many youngsters saw families break up in divorce, etc. They did not feel they belonged; many felt that nobody cared, nobody was interested primarily in them. They want something they didn't have at age 10—they want to be appreciated, accepted, wanted and understood. They want a stabilizing influence, recognition and a sense of belonging. And, Mr. Supervisor, they want it from YOU. You are going to have to give it to them if you want their best efforts on a continuing basis.

You are going to have to influence and inspire these young workers before you motivate them. You could motivate the older employees by threatening to fire them; money was number one on their list of priorities. But—you threaten one of these younger people and they will tell you right quick to "take this job and shove it." And they will take you to the labor board.

There is an EMOTIONAL EXPLOSION in the work force today and the mangement team must deal with it.

I think that the majority of employees through this century will be looking for a lot more than money from their employers. They want personal satisfaction from the job; they are going to have to have respect and recognition.

Management is going to have to "care" about these people, make them feel important, wanted and needed—and provide emotional security along with the pay check. No more harsh, hateful, abrasive, abusive and insensitive treatment of subordinates on the job. Instead, management is going to have to consult with workers and give them a voice in management. I know this will go "against the grain" of some management teams. I am telling it like I see it, like the workers see it, and, if you are reading this book and haven't seen the handwriting on the wall, I hope you will very soon.

Your employees do not mind being "supervised," Mr. Manager, but you must remember you are working with HUMAN BEINGS and the proper way to relate to human beings is with kindness, courtesy, consideration and compassion. If these four words do not describe your techniques in one way or another, I believe they will before long—if you intend to stay in management.

Another Factor

I believe that when you think about the theory of employee value systems as it relates to workers' changing behavior patterns it will make sense to you. But there is another factor even more pertinent in explaining the change in the employee over the years.

Working people are better educated, more knowledgeable and informed than ever. They want jobs they can enjoy and feel excited about. They no longer are willing to accept unrelieved boredom and monotony as inevitable. They want a vital and visible role in the work place and they won't tolerate indifferent and evasive management as something that goes with the territory.

Employees are becoming increasingly aware of their moral and legal rights on the job; they feel these include an open, participative, meaningful and reasonably satisfying relationship with management. This trend of change in employee thinking and expectations is rattling the windows in the board rooms, and well it might. I hope these "labor pains" will bring about the birth of true "industrial democracy" in this country and that an atmosphere of mutual trust, respect and affection will become the norm.

Industrial democracy is not a win/lose proposition. On a job where everybody is equal and where there is a healthy and confidential communication exchange between management and labor, there will be harmony and cooperation and top job performance will be the rule. Everybody wins—the company wins, employees win, consumers win and the community wins. Everybody wins!

The key word is "affection." If team members care about each other, they are more likely to win. Management must take the lead here. Employees are just waiting for the supervisor to extend the olive branch. They are waiting for a more caring relationship with you, so what are you waiting for, Mr. Manager?

The answer is under your nose. You tap your people's spirit by treating ALL OF US like human beings ALL the time.

The cry of management to labor is:

"Why don't you do quality work?

Why don't you cooperate?

Why aren't you loyal?

Why don't you produce?"

Labor is answering back:

"Why don't you treat me like a human being?"

Mr. Supervisor—why don't you?

Management Must Care

The employee wants to feel that the boss CARES about him.

After I spoke to one group of managers, a participant came up and said, "Mrs. Ramsey, I get the feeling that you think all employees are good and all supervisors are bad."

"No, when I talk to employees, I try to tell them what they owe you," I said. Then she began telling me about one of her workers and really was bad-mouthing that person when a friend joined us and started adding to the putdown of the employee.

"You give me the impression that you don't like this employee," I said. She didn't answer and I added, "I get the idea you can't stand this person."

She took a deep breath and stepped back, still not replying, and I told her, "I am sorry, but I have to tell you that if you can't stand this employee you never will motivate her."

Employees need to feel good about you, supervisors; they have to LIKE you and they need to feel that you like them. You can't fake it. This is one of the reasons it takes a special person to be a supervisor.

I was in a group once where a union organizer was trying to get some cards signed. The first thing she said was, "These bosses don't care anything about you. This company doesn't care about your welfare, all it is after is your blood and sweat. Nobody here really cares about you."

A woman in the crowd jumped up and said, "Wait a minute. You are wrong, this company does care about us, too. When my husband was sick, my supervisor came to the hospital, came to my house, sent flowers and one Sunday he brought me a cake. Oh, yes, this company does care about us and you will organize this plant over my dead body!"

Do you see what that employee was doing?

She was judging the entire company by the actions of the first-line supervisor!

Here we must emphasize the importance of the first-line supervisor, that person who is in closest continuous contact with employees every day. This boss doesn't represent the company or organization—he IS the company or organization.

The workers' feelings about the floor boss not only will determine their level of performance, but also their loyalty, or lack of it, to the company to a large degree. The first-line supervisor is the most important person in any organization. He must see his employees not merely as job fillers, but as curious, sensitive, creative individuals who need more from him than orders for the day. Only he can promote a productive-minded, quality-conscious, company-loyal attitude in the work place on a continuing basis. It happens in the nitty-gritty grind on the shop floor, month by month, week by week, day by day, moment by moment.

The first-line supervisor is the lifeline of any operation. A sensitive, positive, caring manner of handling his crew should be his No. 1 priority. Employees do better work for the CARING supervisor.

After I had made this point about "caring" at a chemical company in Alabama, a young supervisor approached me during a break and told me:

"Mrs. Ramsey, what you said about caring is true. I had a young man working for me who obviously was not giving me his best. He was doing mediocre work, just enough to get by, and I tried everything in the book to motivate him.

"I was about ready to give up on him, but about two months ago his grandmother died. I remembered what a trauma it had been for me when my grandmother died so I went to this boy's house and told him to take as much time off as he needed and that I knew how he felt.

"I told him a little about my grandmother and how it had hurt me when she passed away. I told him that if there was anything I could do to help him during this time to let me know. I sent a flower and attended his grandmother's funeral.

"Mrs. Ramsey, that young man came back on the job and you would not have known he was the same person. He is giving me top performance and he is doing the work I knew all the time he could."

You see, supervisors, after everything else in the "book" failed, as soon as the employee realized that his boss really cared about him he went to work.

That's a motivator!

Care about your employees, know what is going on, stand by them when they are hurting. They will repay you in performance.

We have lost a lot of genuine caring in our relationships and we need to get it back.

This is a time of me-ism. It is "get all you can, can all you get, and hide the can." There even is a book out called *Looking Out For Number One.*

You may have heard the story about two fellows running from a bear. One of them started putting on his running shoes and the other said, "No use putting on those running shoes, you're not going to be able to outrun that bear." The other answered back, "I don't have to outrun the bear — all I have to do is outrun YOU!"

This is the prevailing attitude in many work places — "No matter who gets the heat, as long as I don't get it."

The feeling between a worker and his boss SHOULD BE "We share the victories — we share the defeats — we are in this together — we are a team — we care about each other — after any crisis is over, we still will be friends."

There are a lot of ways management can say "we care." I noticed a change in a sign on the wall in my department one day. The old one said: "This department has worked XX number of days without a lost-time accident." The new one said: "This department has worked XX number of days without A DISABLING INJURY." The old sign was company oriented, but the new one said, "WE CARE."

There are many cost-free methods that management can use to get this message across.

Anything that says you care.

If a management person knows in his heart that he never can care about his workers, he should get out of management. Not everybody can handle this aspect of supervising. (See next chapter.)

The 'Toe' Supervisor

I once found a note in my pocket after a speaking engagement which said, "Industry wanted workers and got PEOPLE." Everybody cannot handle people effectively. This is a fact top level management needs to learn. It takes a man or woman of superior intelligence, ability and insight to be a successful supervisor, especially in today's work environment. It takes a capable, caring person of integrity.

One of the biggest problems in labor intensive industries where there are so many supervisors is that a lot of people get into management who never should be there. They can't handle people, never could and never will. They got their jobs because they were somebody's nephew, friend or protege. These misfits in the management structure often stay on in a situation where neither they nor employees are top job performers and they clog up the wheels of production and quality on the job.

I once read a story by Oscar Thompson in which he pictured God looking down on the world and seeing all his human creations as one big person. Some were hands, some fingers, some ears, eyes, etc.

One man was designated a toe and he said to God, "I don't wish to be a toe, I want to be an eye."

"No, go ahead and be a toe," God answered. "That is what I made you."

The man was adamant in his unhappiness and cried, "But I don't want to be a toe."

"I made you a toe and all I expect of you is to be the best toe you can be," God said. "Go ahead and be a good toe."

The man insisted on being an eye, so God finally told him, "All right, go ahead and be an eye—but all you are ever going to see is the inside of a sock."

We have a lot of "Toes" in management and some are trying to be "eyes" but all they can see is the inside of a sock.

You need to BE an EYE to stay in management, not just WANT to be one. It is no disgrace to be a toe. Everybody is not QUALIFIED to handle other people effectively. If you are a toe, just try to be the best one you can be and let the "eyes" do the supervising.

(Now, I know that no one reading this is a TOE, but if you happen to meet one, please tell him what I said.)

One of the cold, hard facts of industry is that some people can be trained in the art of supervision and some can't be. Successful supervisors must be able to APPLY what they learn in management training courses and many great people who mean well and have a sincere desire to manage just cannot make this application. These people never will be effective supervisors.

The Importance Of Practical Application Of Management Techniques

There is no shortage of supervisory training classes. Bosses are sent to management seminars, conferences, forums and conventions on a regular basis. The problem is, they do not bring what they learn back to the shop floor.

A supervisor could go to every training school in the world, go to the library and plow through every book on management and memorize every word in them but, if he could not make a practical application on the shop floor of the things he learned, it is worthless.

We are going to analyze the employee and find out what makes him tick, what motivates and what de-motivates him and look at ways you can make some practical use of the techniques you already know. I fervently hope that you will be able to USE the concepts of shop floor experiences here as we discuss the EMPLOYEE's view on ways you can be:

Confident, but not arrogant;

Supportive, but not over-indulgent.

How you can:

Help without humiliating;

Correct, without condemning;

Be sincere, as opposed to flattering.

How to have:

Friendship, but never familiarity.

And how you can:

Orchestrate, but not dictate on your job.

Show your employees you are emotionally interested IN them, but never become emotionally involved WITH them.

We will explore several areas where the supervisor can

make practical application of his management training, improve the work environment, enrich his relationship with his employees and make everybody's job easier.

But, first, I have two hints for the management team.

Two Hints For Management

When the supervisor walks on the job, he makes two statements before he opens his mouth. His appearance makes a statement and his manner makes another.

The supervisor should, first of all, look like a leader.

Mr. Manager, don't come to work wearing a wrinkled shirt. Remember the "streaking" fad a few years ago when people would take off their clothes and run past a public gathering to startle bystanders? An elderly woman decided to return the compliment to younger streakers by stirring up some excitement on a college campus, so she undressed and "streaked" by a student group.

"What was that?" asked one student.

"I don't know," another answered. "But it needed ironing."

Mr. Supervisor, don't come on the job needing ironing. People will just naturally follow a real leader, but you have to look like one to get their attention. You can't come to work looking like you spent the night upside down in a post hole and think that I am going to follow your leadership. And, there will be no booze breath—you also need to smell like a leader. As a manager, you are a cut above average. Look like it; smell like it—and act like it.

Your manner also makes a statement about you, Mr. Supervisor. You must act like a winner. Nobody does his best work for a loser.

I remember a boss who once took us into a meeting and said, "If we don't get our quality up, they're going to run me off." Employees don't care whether they run you off or not—don't try to get their sympathy. Act confident every minute, have a smile on your face, a sparkle in your eye and a spring in your step. Show you are a winner. Together, we may lose a few battles, but we will win the war. People gravitate toward a winner. Everybody wants to be on the winning team. Winners inspire others to win.

If a boss comes on the job with dirty fingernails and bad breath, shoulders drooping and a furrowed brow, the statements he makes are: I'm careless; I'm sloppy; I'm negligent; I'm afraid I can't do my job; I'm a loser. This is an image today's management cannot afford.

You'll see the following statement repeated many times because it is so important to any effective motivational effort:

"Enthusiasm is not taught—it is caught!"

Act like a winner and employees will catch it.

The boss needs a touch of class and a ton of confidence when he walks on the job—every day. With class and confidence, he is a winner, he is a leader without saying a word. He is trying to be the best he can be.

Being The Best You Can Be

Everyone should have a deep, abiding desire to be the very best person he can be, regardless of his assets, liabilities or station in life. In His wisdom, God made us different and we never should try to imitate anyone else. We should strive to improve upon whatever talent or ability we have been given—or, to put it another way, we should be busy doing the best we can with what we have. This is especially true for the "superior" in the superior/subordinate relationship.

All of us should be moving toward a goal of reaching our full potential in whatever direction our interests and abilities lead us.

Mr. Supervisor, are you trying to be the best boss you can be?

If you are, you surely will be a good example and an inspiration to your employees and they will want to be the best they can be.

You have to be "on the ball" yourself before you can get your workers on it. The boss should have an air of authority and adequacy. His attitude should be "for every problem there is an answer and TOGETHER we will find it." Of course, this is not always easy. We all have moments of anxiety and self-doubt. To keep on keeping on is sometimes like trying to climb a glass mountain with Vaseline shoes on, but it pays to have confidence and keep trying. The prize goes to the person who won't quit.

You may have to TALK TO YOURSELF sometimes, Mr. Supervisor.

The great Enrico Caruso, probably the world's greatest tenor ever, was said to have been heard one time before a performance saying over and over to himself, "You little me, get out of me; you big me, get into me."

Everyone has a feeling of inadequacy at times and, as a supervisor, you have to lecture yourself into getting the "little you" out and force the "big you" to take over. You must show confidence in yourself and your employees.

Babe Ruth was the picture of confidence in a famous scene. It was a pennant game, last inning, last out. His team was three runs behind and the bases were loaded when Babe stepped up to bat. He swung his bat a few times as batters do, then paused and silenced the fans by raising his right hand and pointing toward right field—and over the fence.

Reports were that you could have heard a pin drop as the pitch was delivered and Babe hit it hard, propelling it over the right field wall for a home run. After he trotted home with the winning run, somebody asked, "How did you have the nerve to signal where you would hit the ball? What if you had not followed through?"

"Oh, I never entertained any possibility that I wouldn't do it," the confident Ruth replied.

That was a perfect example of confidence, which pays off in more ways than one. You see, Babe Ruth not only aroused those fans in the stadium, he rattled the pitcher. His opponent no doubt intended to throw a curve, but Babe's display of confidence and self-assurance caused the pitcher to throw a straight ball.

Mr. Supervisor, your employees will not throw you nearly as many curves if you have confidence and display an air of adequacy (but not arrogance) on the job. Arrogance says, "I'm better than you;" confidence says, "I'm going to be the best I can be."

You have reason to be confident—you have earned the right to be in your position. You are "a cut above" and it's okay to take pride in your ability and position. You obviously are just trying to be the best boss you can be.

Employees will accept your authority—we know that the inmates cannot run the asylum. But you have to earn the right to boss us by being "a cut above the average" day in and day out.

Of course, you don't win them all, but you know where you're going and how to persuade others to go with you. When you fall, you jump right back up, like the skater who was asked how he got to be an expert:

"By getting up every time I fall."

The secret is not to give up. Remember the poem about plugging away? The first stanza gives the message:

"It's the plugging away that will win you the day
So don't be a piker, ole pard,
Just call on your grit, it's too easy to quit,
It's the keeping on plugging that's hard."

The story is that Edison failed 1,000 times before he made the light bulb and when somebody told him, "You sure wasted a lot of time," he replied:

"No, I found 1,000 ways NOT to make a light bulb."

Every setback in a person's life, whether he is a supervisor or not, should be a learning and growing experience. Only as we apply this principle can we advance toward our goal—to be the best we can be.

Set your goal—chart your course—make sure your goal is worthy. Play by the rules, go for it! Set your sails, keep your eyes on your goal and you eventually will arrive. You may get off course on occasion, but if your mind is made up and your sails are set, you will come right back. Remember what the poet said, "some ships go east and some go west, while the self same breezes blow; it's the set of the sail and not of the gale that determines the way you will go." A gale may blow one person out of the ball game and that same gale may blow someone else right to the top. It's all according to how our sails are set.

As a supervisor, I hope one of your most desired goals is to maintain a positive relationship with your employees. Remember—a positive relationship is a productive relationship.

Quality Is A Buzz Word In Today's Market Place

As a supervisor, always remember

GOOD WILL
Equals
GOOD WARES
Or
GOOD WORK

I will not give you my best work if I hate your guts. Anybody with the IQ of a box of Fruit Loops ought to know that no one is going to give his best to one he hates.

There must be GOOD WILL on the job. This mutual caring will create a work environment where QUALITY work gets done.

You Can't Make Me Work

Mr. Supervisor, as an employee, one of the first things I want to tell you is that you can't MAKE me work. You have to make me WANT TO WORK.

You may be able to make me work as long as you are watching me, but you can't watch me every minute and if I don't want to work for you, as soon as your back is turned, I will goof off.

Hints, ideas, thoughts and suggestions from the employee perspective ought to be used as fast as you can get them together to make your people "want to" work and do a good job for you. Besides the relationship advantages, they will prevent a situation that can cost you a bundle!

Do you realize that the main reason employees steal, vandalize and destroy company property is because of some real or imagined injustice on the job?

Employees may come to work late, stay out, go home "sick," lay down on the job, or otherwise project a negative attitude and low morale (it's lag, drag, nag) or sign a union card. They will find a way to "get even" when they feel management has not treated them right, or like human beings.

I tell a story in my labor/management talks that graphically illustrates this point:

A group of wealthy people rented a yacht for a cruise to the Bahamas and hired a Chinese boy to cook for them. They took advantage of his inexperience and naïveté and paid him well below scale wage. They didn't show him any respect or acknowledge his efforts to do a good job. They belittled and demeaned him by playing jokes on him. They put tacks in his shoes, emptied ash trays in his bed, laughed at a cake he baked and put him down at every turn.

Later, at their destination, they began to feel sorry for the way they had treated Wong and they told him so.

"Wong," their spokesman said, "we're sorry for the bad way we treated you. After all, you're a human being just like the rest of us. You have feelings and just because we are your employers gives us no right to take advantage of you and discourage you. We are going to make amends. We will pay you the scale wage for cooks and will respect your dignity. And we will not play any more tricks on you."

"Ah," said Wong, "No more ashes in blanket?"

"That's right," answered the spokesman.

"No more tacks in Wong's moccasins?"

"That's right."

"Ah, no more laughee at Wong's cakee?"

"That's right."

"Ah, velly good," said Wong. "No more pee pee in coffee."

Remember, employees will find a way to get even with you for injustice on the job—and they certainly will not "want to" do good work. Many management teams fail to move and motivate their people because they do not even know where the workers' "want to" is located. And many are drinking some bad coffee and don't even know it.

Management must locate, stimulate and activate employees' "want to" by relating to the whole person—not just a pair of hands, but to the whole human being. Ability is not enough anymore. You must have more than your employees' "hands"— you must have their hearts and minds.

YOU CANNOT 'MAKE' A PERSON WORK YOU MUST MAKE HIM 'WANT TO' WORK

Employees are three-dimensional (everybody is) and the WANT TO is not in the hands, but in the heart and mind.

31

Employee

Body	Spirit	Mind
Energy	Emotion	Intellect
Doing	Feeling	Thinking
Action	Enthusiasm	Interest
Skill	**Zeal**	**Will**

'Want To'

Most Labor Relations Problems
     Come From One Basic 'SIN'

Employees Have Three Dimensions,
But Management Only Seems
To Care About One--

What They Are DOING.

Many Times You Don't Care About

How They FEEL

Or

How They THINK!

More Than Hands

As you look at your people, remember every employee is doing three things all day long. He is WORKING—FEELING—THINKING.

Virtually all labor/management problems stem from this one cardinal sin of management.

As the supervisor, you may be interested only in one of the employee's dimensions, what he is doing for you (or his energy). You are concerned only about SKILL. But, skill is not worth much without ZEAL and WILL. Zeal and Will emanate from the HEART and the MIND.

Mr. Supervisor, you have your employee's hands, but most management does not have the hearts and minds of its workers. It only has one-third of the employee's potential—he does only what he absolutely has to do to get by. Remember, the "want to" is NOT in the hands.

If the boss does not consider his people's feelings in his day-to-day dealing with them, their hearts won't be in their work. If he doesn't consider their intelligence, they will not be interested in their jobs.

The result will be poor job performance every time. Following are some ways to get your employees' hearts and minds and, consequently, their best efforts. They are simple, sound and cost-free. And, best of all, they activate and stimulate the workers' "want to."

Now, let's make some shop floor applications.

Recognition!

Let's talk about recognition first. There are dozens of ways you can recognize your people. Everybody likes it—some may not admit it, but everybody likes to be recognized.

Recognition is something we hear a lot about in labor/management discussions on human resources and employee relations these days. One of the things I have observed over the years is that many bosses overlook the importance of basic daily recognition the employee needs for just being there. Just by acknowledging his presence every day will get him off to a good start.

Don't wait until half the day is gone to look at an employee—look at him FIRST THING.

Pay your people a little attention. Remember, this is something most of your employees did not have enough of when they were 10 years old. They want it badly and, if you give it to them, they will pay you back in performance.

Make sure that you don't overlook anyone in the area of recognition, especially those who truly deserve it. This suggestion is extremely important for the first-line supervisor, but all levels of the management structure should read and heed.

A friend told me about a young man who came to work at her plant and turned out to be an outstanding employee in every way. Everybody in the department knew of his good work because if he did not keep his job up, a long row of lights would go on. His lights never were on, his job was being done well.

"George," she asked one day, "has Mr. So and So commended you on the good job you are doing?"

"Mr. So and So never has even spoken to me," he answered.

Mr. So and So was a second-level supervisor who came

through that department every day. Not only had he neglected to notice the good work George was doing, he hadn't even noticed George.

First-line supervisors should acknowledge each employee's presence every day soon after the shift begins. (In the first 15 minutes.) A nod, a smile, a wave of the hand, or a simple hello will do, but don't walk by an employee as if he is a post holding up the ceiling. We are people, human beings, and we deserve a little more attention from you than the building and machinery.

As an employee, I believe that 90 percent of disruptive and counter-productive behavior on the job is nothing more than a cry for attention. Everybody likes attention. We all like to feel we are important in some small way to the success of the operation where we work. Management should not ignore any employee because it wounds a person's pride. To be ignored is that ultimate insult and many will react negatively, causing problems on the job. This type of treatment hurts the employee's *feelings*.

If people in upline management can't smile and speak to employees down in the shop, they should stay out of the shop.

Few things are more demotivating than a big boss strolling through a plant in his fine clothes and his nose in the air. It says to employees, "Big me, little you."

I have seen employees stick out their tongues, make faces and put their middle fingers up (what we call 'shooting a bird') behind the backs of these stiff, cold, arrogant bosses when I knew that, in their hearts, all they really wanted was a kind word, a wave of the hand or some sign of recognition from the "big" boss. Courtesy and kindness are cost free and the super supervisor is courteous and kind to his employees. He acknowledges their presence on the job every day, first thing. He makes them feel important because he thinks they are.

Recognize The Family's Place On His List Of Priorities

Every straight-thinking employee appreciates his job and will cooperate in all ways possible to please management and keep a harmonious relationship. However, management must realize that the job is NOT the No. 1 interest in the employee's life.

The family is No. 1. Please don't ask a worker to put anything ahead of a family emergency.

One night I called my boss and told him I couldn't make it for the third shift because my baby was sick.

"Mildred, I'm sorry. Is it Dougie or Stevie?"

I was stunned momentarily—he knew my children's names!

"I'm so sorry and hope it isn't anything serious," he said. "If there is anything I can do, you know you can call me. Otherwise, I'll look for you when Stevie is better."

Now, that's what I call a super supervisor. I knew he didn't have anybody to take over my job and he knew it, but he never mentioned that because he saw me as a mother first and a weaver next. Know what I did? I found a relative to keep my child the next morning and I was back at the job the next night.

Why? Because my boss stimulated my "want to" when he recognized that my responsibility to a feverish child took precedence over my responsibility to him.

Supervisors who treat their people with kindness and concern in times of family emergency will win, and forever hold, the employee's loyalty and affection. They are relating to their workers in the emotional realm and will activate their "want to."

Remember, people are sensitive about their families.

For example, there was a young mother who sent her son to school for the first time. She was reluctant to let him go, but dressed him up and pinned a note to his lapel. It read:

"Dear Teacher, Johnny is a special child. If he misbehaves, don't hit him. Hit the kid next to him and this will frighten Johnny and he will straighten up."

So, be a super supervisor. Remember your employees' family priorities.

Recognize Ordinary Abilities

Every boss has some employees who never will win any awards. They never will do anything outstanding. These workers need recognition for their ordinary abilities—which get the job done.

One night on a job, a second-level supervisor came up to me and said, "Mildred, I want you to just keep on doing what you're doing."

"What am I doing?" I had no idea what he was talking about.

"I told all the supervisors on third shift to come by your job sometime and see you operate these looms. The way you clean up the waste as you go along is the best way to keep it out of the cloth."

Well, needless to say, I was motivated to do even better because my boss had noticed the way I ran my job and complimented me.

I have wondered many times why management doesn't use this very effective method of positive communication more often. Example—one night the woman who cleaned up—the sweeper—came up, visibly upset.

"Remember the other night when I was out? They had three people doing my job. Don't they know that if it takes three people to do it when I'm out that I've got too much to do? You better believe I'm going to see 'Big Boss' when he comes in tomorrow."

"Why, Janie, honey, you could sweep the whole mill while they sweep the spare floor," I told her. She brightened up and went off smiling. Did she go to "Big Boss"? No—I never heard her mention it again.

Janie needed a little attention. She needed to know that somebody appreciated her ordinary abilities.

Janie was a background person, the kind who never is noticed in a positive way. She "went over the head" of her first-line supervisor with every little complaint. All she really wanted was a little attention.

I wondered again then why management teams overlook so many opportunities to reinforce employees' confidence in themselves and their ability to do a simple job well.

The supervisor who wants to succeed in management will be alert to the unspoken cries for recognition of the Janies on his job and he will make work hours more pleasant for everyone by recognizing the ordinary abilities of his people once in awhile when the opportunity arises.

He will "get" a lot more than he "gives" because this type of supervising stimulates the employee's "want to" and that translates into performance.

Recognize The Employee's Extra Efforts

It really makes an employee feel good about his work when some extra effort he has made is noticed and mentioned by his superiors.

I was asked one time to take a different weaving job—one that was causing a lot of headaches because it was producing a lot of defects in a sheer, hard-to-weave curtain material. I was on the job about a week before one morning I saw the plant manager coming down my alley. He was tall, quite handsome, had big blue eyes and was very kind. He told me he wanted to see me start up one of the curtains.

I showed him how I made the "start up" to prevent a heavy place in the cloth. It was perfect. He rubbed the material and said, "They told me in the cloth room that they could tell a difference in this cloth the night you came on this job."

He walked away and probably forgot what he had said before he had crossed the room, but I NEVER WILL forget it. Why? Because he made me feel good about myself. He made me feel good about my peers who had mentioned my work to him and good about him as a plant manager and about the company. He activated my "want to" and I said to myself as he disappeared, "You handsome, blue-eyed rascal you, you ain't seen nothing yet." He made me want to do an even better job!

Let's analyze this little episode which meant so much to me that I remember it vividly after 30 years. First of all, what the manager did was simple, nothing deep or hard to figure out —SIMPLE. Second, it was sincere. What he said was true, not flattery. Third, and most important, it was SPECIFIC. Supervisors shouldn't tell an employee "You're doing a good job and I appreciate it." That isn't worth a feather in a whirlwind, because we all know you probably say it a dozen times a day.

If I'm doing a good job and you appreciate it, what was it I did that impressed you? Tell me THAT and I never will forget it. Be specific when communicating with one individual. A general statement by the supervisor congratulating a group as a team is all right, but generalities are not remembered and they do not motivate.

The truly super supervisor will keep his eyes open for extra efforts and he will recognize each effort in a simple, sincere, specific manner. (This is positive reinforcement.) He will praise each of his people at least a couple of times a year in some special way. My plant manager never spoke to me individually except that one time, but it was enough. He made me feel important—feel good about myself and my peers—and I never forgot. Employees who are mistreated never forget and those who are appreciated never forget. This is not spoiling—it is REINFORCEMENT.

There is something in it for you, Mr. Manager, if you treat your people like human beings. Recognize their daily presence on the job. Recognize their ordinary efforts and recognize them for extra and outstanding performance. Recognition on the job makes employees "want to" give their best. REINFORCE-MENT WORKS!

Reinforce Positive Behavior
Of Employees

Somebody handed me a card at a meeting which read: "The reinforcement of desired behavior will eliminate undesired behavior."

When I read that, I thought of an incident a few years ago when a great friend of mine called one day to tell me of some unexpected good work by a trainee—and a missed opportunity by their supervisor.

Seems one of my friend's looms got fouled up and made such a mess she called the supervisor in despair. He brought over a young trainee and gave her the job of fixing it. (Oh, Lord, a trainee to fix that mess, my friend thought.) The trainee had the loom running better than ever in a short while and the weaver showed the boss what a good job the young employee had done, hoping he would pass along some praise.

But, the boss never mentioned it to the trainee.

He struck out with an older employee and a new one in one swing when he could have hit a home run with both of them. He could have won the trainee's respect for life, for the job and for the company. He should have gone to the young worker and said, "Delores, Sandra told me what a great job you did on her loom. If that's a sample of your work, I can't wait to get you trained and on your own job here."

He could have made Delores feel good about her peer, about him and about herself. He thoughtlessly turned down an opportunity handed him on a platter.

Supervisors, watch your people, notice what they are doing. Reinforce the positive things they do. You will find that it is true that reinforcement of desired behavior eliminates undesired behavior.

Reinforcement of desired behavior is much more than the theory learned in schooling, writing, talking and thinking. Practical application is what management needs to concentrate on—apply all that theory to your people in a practical manner. Take the case of Juanita, who on a particular day was in definite need of a reinforcement of attitude.

Juanita was angry at her supervisor about one of the various job problems in which she felt her view was being overlooked and she was stalking the boss this day.

"I'm going to tear that guy up when he comes by here," she vowed, keeping an eye on the office.

But the wise supervisor could tell which way the wind was blowing and he put a practical application of behavioral reinforcement on her. Approaching her area, he greeted her and said, "There's something I've been meaning to tell you."

That stalled her planned outburst and he continued:

"Everybody appreciates how clean you keep your area and I never hesitate to bring visitors by your job when we are showing off our operation."

Then he put on the clincher:

"I'll bet you are a good housekeeper at home, too."

That did it—he made her feel good about herself on the job and off—a positive, practical application of a mountain of theory.

Juanita took the desired approach with him also—they talked about her problem a few minutes and he left—not "torn up," but a super supervisor, with a positive-minded worker.

Reinforcement of desired behavior WILL eliminate undesired behavior.

Recognize That Subordinates Are Programmable

Program and re-program employee computers (minds) with positives.

Bad attitudes can be altered. Counter-productive habits can be changed. Feelings of disloyalty can be reversed. These negatives are all in the mind. As a supervisor, you are a computer programmer whether you have studied the science or not.

You are programming your people's minds with positives or negatives every day. Between the ears of each of your employees is a magnificent computer. If it could be reproduced outside the human skull, someone has said it would cover 10 acres of space and cost $10 billion. This is what you have under your control eight hours a day, five or six days a week. What a challenge!

As a supervisor, you should be dropping in productive programs, good things about the company, pride in accomplishment, joy in a job well done, rewards of self-discipline, group pride or team spirit, individual recognition and any and all positive job-related ideas and suggestions.

The power of suggestion is stronger than most people ever realize. What a shame, and, yes, a disgrace, when often after employers have worked day in and day out for years with their employees and outsiders can come in and within two months steal them away. We all have seen this happen and it never should happen—and wouldn't—if management only would become acquainted with ALL the dimensions of their workers and orient them toward loyalty and unity and program them positively with "upbeat" thoughts and ideas.

All attitudes originate in the mind, even though they are developed in the heart. If you have an employee who is hostile, sloppy and unproductive, it's because somebody has programmed his mind along the way with negatives. Thought patterns can be revised, rearranged and replaced. It may take a little time, but you will get the desired read-out someday if you are determined to win your workers' minds through positive thought programming, whether they are brilliant, illiterate, or somewhere in between.

I know some boss is thinking, "What can you do if you get one of those computers which somebody else has messed up before you get it?" Well, I'm happy to tell you that you can RE-PROGRAM a messed-up computer, IF one condition is present. Take the case of Merrill, a young man who was lazy, belligerent, unproductive and totally disinterested in job performance.

This fellow was pointed out to me one night by a supervisor who had despaired at getting anything out of him. The boss had tried him at every task, but said, "He just won't do anything. He ain't worth a __ __ __ __."

"Have you tried bragging on him?" I asked. That stopped the supervisor cold and he returned the question, "What in the world would I brag on?" "A hard look might reveal some tiny something," I replied. The boss pointed a finger at me:

"Let's see YOU find something."

Well, I looked and admit it was a tough case. The young man had three heads of hair! I never saw so much hair on one head and he had enough necklaces around his neck to sink a whale. Worse, he had narrow black eyes that said clearly, "Leave me alone."

Trying to find a way to approach him, I learned his name was Merrill. One night I walked up to him and said, "Son, they tell me your name is Merrill."

"That's right."

"You know, that's a beautiful name. I like it. I imagine that when you were born and your mother gave you that name she must have thought you would grow up to be a kind and sensitive man. That is not an ordinary name, but of a special kind of person."

I felt I had touched him slightly, because he gave me a small smile. The next day I wrote a poem about his name. He loved it and began to talk to me a little, revealing that he had reason to be mad at the world. His boyhood had been torn apart by those who should have been caring for him and he got in trouble. He was on what authorities call "work release," a prisoner by day, a textile employee by night.

As Merrill warmed up to my overture of friendship, I realized that God had given me a golden opportunity to help this lonely young man. I began to program his computer with positives. I praised him when he did a good job of mopping up around my machines. He responded by working his head off. I talked to him about job performance, working regularly, the importance of a job in relation to a person's self-image, sense of accomplishment, feelings of self-worth. I shared with him many of my own experiences and, as I dropped various positives into Merrill's computer, I saw a change taking place.

One night I said, "Merrill, I like your hair myself, but I believe the younger girls would like it better short. You don't see many Afros anymore." I never intended to mention it again, but about three days later he came to work with a short haircut.

A year or so after I left the weave room for another department, I looked up one day and Merrill was standing in the door—clean as a pin, hair cut neatly—and he had on ONE necklace!

Most youths on work release would quit the mill the same day their jail sentences were up, but I had urged Merrill not to do that, but to stay on the job while he decided what to do in the future. It made me happy that he had taken my advice, had been working every day and had been given a better job. I cried after he left, recalling the first time I saw him and what his attitude had been.

I believe that anyone can change the wrong attitude of another person and, supervisors, you can take a negative-thinking, unproductive misfit and make him a productive-minded, quality-conscious, fiercely-loyal employee—IF YOU

45

CARE. You may not have much to start with. All I had was Merrill's name. It may take a while, but, oh, think what the outcome will be, not just for you and the job, but for the individual in all his relationships through life.

So, supervisors, program those thought patterns with positives! Re-program those messed-up computers. You've got plenty of time—you're with those employees one-third of their lives. Care about your workers and don't be afraid to show it. Keep those computers humming with proud, productive and positive programs. Proud, productive and positive results will be your reward.

You can't program a computer with negatives and get positive read-outs.

Recognize The Employee's Feelings

This is the most important point I will make in this book. The employee's feelings, or his heart, is the doorway to the rest of him.

If you want a worker to invest more energy in his job, you will have to go through this door. If you want him to upgrade his performance, you will have to go through his heart's door. If you want him to make a commitment to excellence on the job, you must reach him through this same door.

Think about the body as a state, say South Carolina. The head may be Charleston, the feet may be Greenville and the hands may be Spartanburg, but the heart is Columbia. This is the capital city. This is where the decisions are made that govern the rest of the state. This is where laws are passed, this is headquarters. (The emotions.)

For this reason, it is very important for the supervisor to consider his employees' feelings on the job every chance he gets.

I once worked with a man named John, a loom fixer who was always talking about a boss he had at another place. "Old Joe was the best boss that ever lived. I would have done anything for him," John would say, or "I would have worked my tail off for him," always praising his former boss. I often wondered what this supervisor had done for John and one night he told me.

John's mother had died after a long bout with cancer. Several times during her illness, John found it necessary to be off from work for a few days. The first time, he was not working for Joe, but had another boss, Bill. When John returned after being off, Bill greeted him:

"John, I'm sure glad to see you back, that job has been in the floor ever since you've been out. I sure hope you don't have to be off anymore."

Time went on and John was moved to Joe's job and his mother's health got worse and he had to miss several more days of work. The day he got back, Joe was waiting for him at the plant steps, shook his hand, and said, "John, I'm sure glad to see you back—how's your mother?"

"How's your mother?" That's what this boss had done for John that made him willing to do anything for him.

Now, Bill had been a good boss and liked John, saw him as a good employee and missed him when he was out. But Joe saw John as a hurting human being who was losing the best friend he ever would have in life, his mother, and he asked, "How's your mother?"

Both these bosses wanted the same thing out of John. They both wanted his energy—but Joe got it because he went through the right door, John's emotions, or his heart. Not only did Joe get top job performance from John on a continuing basis, he made a friend for life. He saw John as a person first and a loom fixer second. This is what all employees want from the boss. This is what we mean when we say we want to be treated like "human beings."

The supervisor who remembers this and acts accordingly will reap bountifully in performance because he will get RESPONSE instead of REACTION and his employees will work their "tails off" for him.

Recognize And Utilize Employees' Intelligence

The Super Supervisor will find ways to compliment his employees' intelligence, even if some are not educated. This boss will not treat one of his workers like he was stupid, but will utilize whatever mental capacity each person has in job-related activities.

I once worked with a young man named Ron, who had very little education. We kept cards on the machines showing defects, etc., and each card was dated. When a month ended, Ron would keep on numbering, 30, 31, 32 and so on. He did not know how many days a month has.

One morning this educationally-disadvantaged employee had a machine that was not running. Different people came from all over the place to try to fix it. There was a crowd around all morning trying different ways to get it running and two or three times I saw Ron go up to them with a suggestion, but his supervisor shooed him away—"Go on, run the other looms, we'll fix this one. Go on." But they had not fixed it by noon and I saw the plant manager coming, You know how they walk—all stiff and straight like a drill sergeant, with arms folded. (I often wondered why they do that—do they think it looks important, or are they hugging themselves?) Mr. Manager bent over the machine, thinking he would scare it, I guess, but it didn't work, so he disappeared as big bosses do and his lower level bosses followed, as they also are known to do, and the loom hadn't hit a lick.

Then, I saw Ron walk over to it—and you know the rest. Thirty minutes later he had it humming and it kept running all day. Ron was lacking in education, he did not know how many days a month has, but he had an intellectual contribution to make to the job—one that his boss failed to recognize.

I think the supervisor should have gone to Ron first thing and said, "Ron, you run this loom every day and probably know it better than the man who designed it. I'm going to put somebody else on your job for a while and you see if you can fix it."

Even if he was unable to fix the loom, think what the supervisor's action would have done for an educationally-disadvantaged employee! And for Ron's work attitude and "want to."

You see, Ron was not educated, but he was not stupid.

Many employees, especially those in labor intensive industries, are lacking in formal education, but they are intelligent and alert and they have ideas, suggestions and know-how that could help solve a lot of management's problems if they were treated as three-dimensional persons and not just as mindless "job fillers."

Mr. Manager, get your people's minds.

We have heard the saying, "Whatever gets your mind, gets you." Make your workers feel important, make them feel included, make them feel needed by recognizing and utilizing their intelligence on the job, no matter how limited it may be. The successful manager of the future will encourage all employees to use their mental capacities as well as physical ones. He will alter all arrogant, indifferent and insensitive attitudes toward workers and treat them as he would wish to be treated. When the Golden Rule becomes the Management Rule, employees will thaw out and respond and top job performance will become the norm.

Mr. Supervisor, your employee's interest in his work will emanate from his mind. If you have an employee who is not interested in his job, it is your fault. Ask your people some questions once in awhile. Don't always talk to them in declaratives. Say to each employee occasionally, "Give this some thought." Let him know you are aware of his mind. You may be surprised at how much these people can help you on the job.

When you talk to him and ask him questions—and listen to him—you make an employee feel he "belongs." A person will be loyal to something he belongs to. The weirdest idiot in town will not act against himself. The reason workers vote for a union is they do not feel they "belong"—if they did belong, they would not vote against themselves. Nobody does that.

It is your job, Mr. Supervisor, to make every one of your employees feel they are an important part of your operation, that they belong to the team. The way to do this is through recognition of, and consideration for, the two dimensions you cannot see—the heart (feelings) and the mind (the intellect).

I remember another incident involving an elderly man who was a sweeper. He couldn't read or write, had no formal education, but he made a living sweeping the mill floor. That was about all that was expected of him. Then came a day when a frame that moved yarn from one place to another broke down. It would run awhile, then stop and nobody could find out why.

The problem continued for several days and it had everybody in the department stumped. It was bugging the supervisor to distraction. The old sweeper went around to the front of the frame during one breakdown and asked the operator if the problem still had him puzzled.

"I'm still having trouble, but I don't think you can do anything to help me," said the operator.

"Well," said the sweeper, "maybe I shouldn't even mention it, but every day when I sweep behind your frame I notice a small break in the cable when it passes through that little open space."

You can guess the rest of the story. Even an old man who couldn't write his name had an intellectual contribution to make.

I asked the supervisor who told me about this, "Did you praise that sweeper for helping solve your problem?"

"No, but I bought him a Pepsi."

UGH!!

Every employee should be encouraged to speak out with suggestions and ideas—and always to speak up when something is amiss. It makes them feel they are an important part of the operation and makes them "want to" please you and do a good job every day they work for you.

Everybody benefits when a SUPER supervisor is on the job. He considers every employee an individual able to make a contribution to the benefit of all—and the company, too.

Never Insult An Employee's Intelligence

I went to work one day with an idea about a problem we were having and approached my supervisor.

"You know those seconds (defects) we have been having with that nylon seersucker? Well, I've been thinking . . ." He cut me off in mid-sentence:

"Nobody's paying you to think. Go on over there and run your job."

NO! NO!, management team. Be careful that you never insult a worker's intelligence.

I said to myself, "You turkey, you may not be paying me to think, but I am thinking anyway and it would not do for you to know what I am thinking right now."

This boss did not mean to hurt my feelings. He liked me and we got along all right. He was busy and didn't have time to talk to me. He forgot what he had said before I was out of sight. But it cut me to the quick and I never forgot it.

Supervisors, don't push your employees aside and ignore their efforts to share thoughts, ideas and suggestions with you. Listen to your people—when you do, you are complimenting their intelligence, whether you use their ideas or not, and they will follow you to the jumping off place.

Be careful—NEVER insult an employee's intelligence.

One-half of my "want to" is located in my mind.

Don't Make Comparisons

Do not compare one employee unfavorably with another. Each worker must be motivated to reach his own potential. Don't say, "Johnny, why can't you do as well as Ronnie?"

Johnny is not Ronnie. Everyone is beautiful in his own way. Johnny needs to feel good about his own ability, not Ronnie's. When bosses make comparisons, they get "reaction" from employees instead of the "response" they are seeking.

This is a technique that is used a lot—and it stinks. Sometimes it is used in families and other relationships, but it always stinks. You can't motivate a person by putting him down. It never will work in the long run. You may make someone angry by comparing him unfavorably with his peers and this may produce a spurt of energy for a short time, but when the "mad" wears off, the spurt sputters and the employee is looking for a way to mess up your coffee.

Mr. Supervisor, when you put Johnny down by telling him he is not as good as Ronnie, he will not think much of you—and not too much of Ronnie, either. You have made him feel bad about himself, about his co-worker and about you. I am amazed that anybody on earth could think it possible to get people's best efforts through such negative methods.

Don't talk "down" to me, Mr. Supervisor, talk "up" to me. Don't put me "down," put me "up." Don't be a downbeat boss, be an upbeat boss. Talk to me about MY accomplishments, not somebody else's. Tell me something I did well, not something somebody else did. What good points do I have, Mr. Bossman? I am not interested in another's good points. Mention MINE when you are communicating with me. When you talk to Ronnie, tell him about his good work, but don't tell me about it if it is better than mine.

Honest praise is the granddaddy of all motivators. Find something to praise your workers for TODAY. If they did not do such a hot job today in one area, look at some other angle—there is something you can say a good word about; so, do it and tomorrow they will do a hot job for you. IT WORKS!

Your employee needs to feel good about himself;

He needs to feel good about his peers;

He needs to feel good about YOU.

Don't make him feel inferior. Make him stand out.

Inferior people do inferior work. Outstanding people do outstanding work.

Use Your Authority Quietly

As employees, we need to feel good about each other. Don't haul me up short in front of my peers. We need and respect your authority, but don't come into the break area after me; don't send another employee in the the restroom for me; don't haul me off to the office in front of other workers.

I have seen supervisors practically drag employees off the floor to the office, making a big show of their authority, as others stood by and watched. Some would laugh and make motions like they were cutting their throats or hanging themselves as the harried employee passed them. The boss would have a thundercloud expression and be walking fast, hurrying the poor subject of his ire along red-faced and humiliated.

If you want to see me in the office, come and quietly inform me and you go back a different route and I'll meet you there. In the first place, supervisors should do as little of this as possible, and eliminating it altogether would be a good idea. Don't do anything on the job that makes me look bad in the eyes of my co-workers.

I was in the restroom one night and the supervisor sent a worker to get me. "He's mad as ＿ ＿ ＿ ＿," she said. Several of us were there taking a break and the rest got quiet and looked at me with pity and embarrassment, some a little gloatingly because it wasn't them being sent for.

I went back on my job and the boss was gone. He had found an end running loose on one of my looms. A thread had broken and was not running in the cloth where it should, but was piling up on the floor. It apparently had been running undetected for some time. I saw a crowd near this loom, all laughing. The supervisor had pulled all the loose thread from under the loom and laid it on top where everybody could see it. It was a huge wad and, as the others jeered about my obvious lack of proper inspecting, I felt stupid and inadequate in front of them.

Mr. Supervisor, don't do things on the job that make your people feel stupid and inadequate. Employees with these feelings do not perform well and they will hate you for hauling them up short before their peers.

The incident of the "loose end" happens often in the weave room and I couldn't help comparing this particular boss with another one in a similar situation. That time my boss waited until I returned from my break and said, "Mildred, I found an end running out on loom 1430. I put it back in the cloth and started your loom up so you wouldn't lose your production, but you might want to have the fixer check the stop motion."

I went to loom 1430 and found that the end had been running out for a long time, but I couldn't find the loose thread. My nice boss had destroyed it to spare my feelings.

I loved him. I felt bad about the ruined cloth, but I did not feel stupid or inadequate.

Now, which one of these bosses do you think got my best efforts?

The super supervisor will not abuse his authority and will not embarrass his employees in front of others and his people will love him for it and do a better job for him.

Remember, industry wanted workers and got people. Dignity is "in" these days on the job.

The 'Worship Me' Boss

Some supervisors have a "worship me" complex. They like to see workers scrape and bow and show an attitude of reverence toward them. They always inspire fear in their people as they remind them in hundreds of little ways that, as bosses, they hold the employees' economic welfare in their hands.

When this type distributes the paychecks, he acts as if they were coming out of his own pocket. He expects his employees to jump when he appears and he likes to make somebody cry now and then. There aren't too many of this type left, but there are some.

Nobody wants to be put in the position of having to stand in awe of another human being, certainly not a flawed, fault-filled one like a boss on a job. The employee is willing to respect you, but he does not want to worship you.

Come down off your high horse, Mr. Supervisor, the air is thin up there and you'll probably be by yourself. Your workers never will "want to" do a good job for you in an atmosphere of apprehension and tension.

New supervisors and management trainees, don't ever succumb to the temptation to "lord it over" employees. This type of bossing may backfire on you and blow you right off the management team.

Bosses, Introduce Yourselves

A new second-level manager, or "boss weaver" for three weave rooms, was hired at my plant one time and about two weeks later I heard two co-workers talking about him and asked how they liked him as a boss.

"We don't know," one answered, "The stuck up turkey hasn't even spoken to us." The other added: "He can't be bothered with us peasants."

A new boss should speak to and shake hands with every employee the first day. Keep in mind, we are all equal, we just have different roles. We are all on the same team, just playing different positions. Nothing is more important to a new boss than getting off to a good start with ALL his people. (I found out later that this particular boss had introduced himself to all the young, pretty women—the old, homely ones were mad.)

That's no attempt at humor—that's true, and, Mr. Manager, you are going to need the support of ALL employees to do a top job. So, when you go on a new position, introduce yourself and shake hands with everyone there—the old and ugly can ruin your effectiveness as a supervisor.

Everybody is equal and everybody is important on the super supervisor's job.

Stop Being A Hypocrite

"Take that weaver to the office and give her hell."

I was reading the lips of my top-level supervisor, who was talking to my immediate boss. The weave room machines make a loud roar and you can't hear very much, so employees there learn early to read lips.

The "boss weaver" came on down my way (not knowing I had read his lips) and was very kind and considerate, asking about my disabled husband, and could not have been more solicitous. He even mentioned my good work. Sugar wouldn't have melted in his mouth. When he left, my first-line supervisor came after me, took me to the office and gave me hell. I was the weaver the big boss was talking to him about, as I suspected.

Next time I saw Mr. Big, I thought, "You hypocritical old turkey, why can't you be honest with your employees? Why put your dirty work off on the straw boss? You're not fooling anybody."

I wondered then, and thousands of times since, why can't labor and management get along? Why not level with each other and really care about each other? And, I'm still wondering.

Although nobody gives anybody as much hell these days and labor/management relationships definitely have improved in the 20 years since this incident, most employees I talk to still feel the management team is too secretive, evasive and hypocritical in dealing with workers. They feel that way especially toward upline management.

Mr. High Boss, don't tell Mr. Low Boss to give workers hell and by no means pass along such instructions on the job. A worker might read your lips and become turned off for 20 years.

Listen To Your Employees

The bulletin board is not an effective means of communicating with your work force.

A large percentage of workers never look at bulletin boards. Of those who do, many do not understand how the message there pertains to them personally. Communication is an EXCHANGE of thoughts, ideas, opinions and suggestions. Employees can't exchange thoughts, ideas, opinions and suggestions with a bulletin board. They surely can't cooperate with it.

The first rule of cooperation is "listening."

When management tells a worker what to do and he does it, that is not cooperation, that is dictation. Most supervisors are likely to use the dictation method in employee relations. It most often falls way short of obtaining maximum results.

A few years ago, a young unionist came to North Carolina from New York and was having phenomenal success organizing workers in this formerly fiercely anti-union area. She was winning elections by wide margins and nobody could figure it out. Asked what her secret was, she had a simple answer: "I listen." All she had to do was park at the plant gate, jump up on her car hood and "listen" to employees, agree with them and sign them up.

Mr. Supervisor, how much do you listen to your people? If you won't take the time to listen to them, there always is someone who will.

Give Employees A Few Minutes Of Your Undivided Attention

During 42 years as an employee, I would like to have said a lot of things to a lot of bosses:

Don't talk to me on the run. Stop, look me in the eye and tell me what you have to say. I can't hear or understand you as you rush by and shout at me.

Don't talk too fast. Don't chatter like a monkey with its mouth full of marbles. Slow down. I didn't do what you asked me to because I didn't hear or understand what you said.

Don't interrupt me when I am talking to you. Don't cut me off in mid-sentence.

Don't change the subject. These things infuriate me. Infuriated workers don't produce.

If the Big Boss walks up, don't turn away from me and start talking to him. Let HIM wait. If he has any class, he will give you a commendation for this. Don't leave me standing with my face hanging out—let me finish and then see what the Big Guy wants.

If he and I were away from the plant four days at the same time, which one of us would you miss the most?

I have spoken several times at a food processing plant which has a great lady as training instructor. Once when I was there, a group was about to make a tour of the plant when one of her part-time workers ran up and asked if the instructor could find something for her to do.

The instructor just turned her back on us and talked to the girl, asking if she could run a copying machine, finally telling her to go to the office and get the man there to show her how. Some VIPs and I stood by while the question was given due consideration—and an answer.

I have heard about great employee relations at this plant and it became clear how they were established. The young part-time employee was wearing a white uniform and black rubber boots required in the production end of the plant, but this wise instructor didn't hesitate to send her to the office to learn a job.

A lot of supervisors would have pushed the employee aside saying, "Can't you see I am busy? I have visitors. Can't you see I'm conducting a tour? Don't bother me now." But not this world class manager—she cares about her employees.

This training instructor was interested primarily in preserving the employee's dignity. The visitors were not the important figures—SHE was.

Supervisors, your relationship with your workers is your most important consideration. They are the ones who are going to do the job. They will make you look like mediocre leaders or they will make you look like experts, depending on their personal relationship with you, or how they FEEL about you. Work closely with them in the emotional realm.

Give your employees a few minutes of your undivided attention once in a while.

It's cheap insurance.

Giving Employees A 'Voice' In Management

Employees do not wish to run the store.

I do not mean that employees should be consulted about choosing the chairman of the board, when to liquidate assets, or when to acquire new plants. I am talking about allowing workers to have some "say so" about little things involving them personally on the job. You may not allow your child to pick out the furniture for his room, but you could let him help you arrange it.

You want output? Okay, then give me some input! Let your employees help you set up the guidelines they will be expected to follow every day of their lives on the job.

Involve them in the policies and procedures of on-the-job conduct as much as possible—not COMPANY policy; find ways every day to let your people participate in whatever is "going on" on your job, something "on the side" or different from what they do all the time. Examples:

Safety committee, coffee club, flower club, blood bank, employee advisory committee, suggestion box committee, welcome new people committee, employee information and education committee (this committee would report on positive things about the company or organization.)

The list is endless, but the smart supervisor will enlist his employees—all of them—in some project on the job every month or so. That brings their personalities into the picture.

The participation principle *produces*.

Let's say you have a problem employee. Tomorrow morning you go up to this worker and hand him the key to the first aid cabinet and tell him, "Sam, you are going to be my first aid man for this month. Anybody who wants anything out of the cabinet has to come to you; you unlock the cabinet, give them

64

what they need, write down what they get and lock the cabinet. At the end of the month, I will come get the key and the list, but you are in charge until then."

I guarantee you will see a difference in this employee's attitude and his performance. Why? You have made him feel good about himself—he's important—he is participating in management in a small way. It MOTIVATES and stimulates his "want to."

So, draw a circle and take them in.

Everybody is somebody on your job. Don't leave anybody standing out in the cold.

Look for ways to endear your employees to you and your organization. Try to enrich your relationship with them by including each one in job-related programs and activities from time to time and by treating them all as equals. Try to draw each worker into some area where the personality is involved. This makes a person feel like an "insider," and not an "outsider." Give everyone some input. I took the liberty of using a line or two I found in a book and wrote a poem about the results of leaving an employee "out."

MY BOSS

He drew a circle and left me out,
My boss was a negative, insensitive lout;
Together we had the stuff to win
But he was unwilling to take me "in."
The enemy saw that I was free,
He drew a circle and beckoned me;
I had no wish my boss to flout
But I went because he left me out.

Take all of your people into a magic circle called industrial democracy. Belonging energizes, it excites and it MOTIVATES.

Build Employees' Self Esteem

Mr. Supervisor, building up your employees' confidence in you is not the best thing you can do—the best thing you can do is build up their confidence in themselves.

A person's self image will determine the kind of job he will do. Make him think he is good and he will get good. Make him think he is getting better and he will get better. Make him think he can do great wonders and he will work his "tail" off to prove you right.

Don't ever make a worker feel inadequate for the task at hand. Don't make him think he cannot do it. The poet was right when he said:

> If you think you are beaten, you are;
> If you think that you dare not, you don't;
> If you'd like to win, but don't think you can,
> It's a pretty good bet that you won't.
> Life's battles are not always won
> By the stronger or smarter man
> But you'll find in the end
> The one who will win
> Is the person who thinks that he can.

Make an employee think he can do great things and he won't disappoint you. Inspire your people to have confidence in themselves.

Mr. Supervisor, if you make a worker feel good about himself, you won't have to worry, he certainly will feel good about you and will "want to" do a super job.

Remember—the body is a puppy dog, it follows the mind. Program your subordinates' minds positively and their bodies will RESPOND positively. So, supervisors, build up employees' confidence in themselves.

Relate To Employees In Terms
Of Their Needs

Base your relations with employees on consideration of their needs. Also:

Of their wants;

Of their feelings;

Of their future;

Of their self-worth.

What is in it for me, Mr. Supervisor, if I do what you ask me to do?

One of the things missing in many work places today is a commitment to excellence, that good feeling of accomplishment and joy in a job well done. We need to get this back and I believe the way to do it is for supervisors to make employees feel worthy and important. Most workers really want to do good work, but have been made to feel that "what's in it for the company" is the primary concern and is not to be shared.

It should be brought to the attention of the work force regularly that a thriving and prosperous business means thriving and prosperous employees.

There is something in it for the worker when top job performance is the norm in his work place, something more than hard work and pay. Instill in each employee the deeply satisfying feeling of achievement and well being that he needs to keep his interest up in a job that may be repetitious and monotonous.

My little grandson came for a visit one day while I was writing this book and sat on the stairs banging his head back and forth on the bannister. Bang. Bang. Bang.

"Stevie, stop that noise, Granny is trying to concentrate," I said.

Bang. Bang. Bang. He didn't even slow down. I started to say, "Cut out that noise or I'm going to bang your other end," but I thought for a moment and said instead:

"Stevie, baby, you'd better stop that. You are going to hurt that sweet little head of yours."

Not another bang.

The moment I explained what was in it for him, he stopped.

What's in it for me, Mr. Supervisor, if we run a top job? A secure future? A job for my children someday? Self pride? Promotion? (Those are excellent computer program topics!)

Mention these things to us once in awhile and we will regain a commitment to excellence and everybody in our operation will benefit.

Your Employee Is Your Equal, He Just Has A Different Role

Don't talk "down" to employees.

Don't yell, don't make motions, don't whistle.

If you want to tell a worker something, walk up to him and speak in a normal voice. He understands English.

The supervisor-subordinate factor is ever present. If I am your employee, I know that you are my superior on the job and I am your subordinate. I knew it before I left home this morning. But don't rub it in. Don't let your actions send the message: Big me, Little You.

I have heard hundreds of employees say after a pow wow with the boss, "I'll tell him right now, I'm just as good as he is." Anytime a supervisor leaves an employee with this reaction, he has made a mistake. The employee IS as good as he is—we are all equal, just in different roles. The lowest paid sweeper is equal to the company president as a person. So, unless you yell, motion or whistle at the company president, don't yell, motion or whistle at the sweeper. Talking "down" to a person demotivates him.

Don't make careless statements. Think before you approach a worker. Is what you are about to say going to encourage him? If not, we all would be better off if you didn't say anything. Think before you speak to anyone and you may prevent a lot of hostility and embarrassment.

We often are like the man at a party who noticed an unattractive woman enter the room and said to the man next to him, "I wonder who that ugly woman is."

"That's my wife," the man answered.

"Lord help both of us—you ought to see mine," the embarrassed observer continued quickly.

That was a quick thinking effort to cover up—but thinking

FIRST would have been much better.

Mr. Supervisor, every time you approach an employee you must visualize a feeling, thinking, emotional human being who needs encouragement from you. Weigh your words carefully. A discouraged person is a demotivated person and employee.

The wrong words can paralyze.

Massive doses of encouragement will stimulate, motivate and activate people. And it is cost-free.

Don't Talk Over
Your Employees' Heads

Some management teams use "lawyer" talk when communicating with their employees, especially in group meetings.

I have attended hundreds of these meetings since 1942 and almost every time when we would come out, someone would ask, "What was that all about?"

I remember once getting back to my work area after a briefing on insurance by a speaker who had the personality of a dial tone. A group of co-workers awaited me and one said, "I told them to come down here and you would explain to us what all that meant."

Management Team, don't talk over your people's heads. First of all, be sure the speaker is someone who speaks clearly and whose voice is pleasant. Speak loudly, a lot of older employees don't hear so well anymore. If the group is large, don't stand on the same level as the audience; a lot of us depend on lip reading to help us hear—we have to be able to see you. Direct your remarks to the least educated person in the room; if he understands, the others will. Many industries still have large numbers of educationally disadvantaged, so I would say when management calls employees together to explain some policy, plan or procedure, speakers should make their messages plain enough for a grammar school student to understand. After all, if your people don't know what you said, you have just wasted a lot of time.

When you talk over our heads, you make us feel stupid and not much is expected of stupid employees in the way of performance.

Be Your Employees' Friend

What is a friend? One of the definitions of "friend" is a person who favors and supports another. Another is a person on the same side. We can interpret these to mean people involved in the same struggle and supporting each other.

What struggle are labor and management involved in? We are in a struggle to produce a quality product or service that we can sell at a competitive price.

Those paychecks do not fall from Heaven on Friday. We must produce something and sell it before the payroll can be met. We must produce a lot of it and it must be better and cheaper than the product of our competitors.

Management Team, keep this fact before your employees every day of the year. Put it in those computers. It's the name of the game. It's a constant struggle. Never ending. It's our JOB. If you are struggling alongside friends, it's a whole lot easier for everybody.

A Sign For Every Department

The only chance we have to survive Is IF we WORK HARDER than the Competition!!

Plan Employee Education Classes

Every work place should have a program of continuing education for employees, as well as for management.

Most workers do not know enough about the operation which they are expected to support and invest their energy and years of their lives in. Employee education classes are an excellent way to keep your people informed about the company or organization. Every good and positive action you have undertaken, past, present or future, should be studied in detail by every employee. (An in-house newsletter is another good way.)

Classes can be short one-day or one-hour seminars or continuous courses, depending upon the subject. Enlighten your employees, tell them everything you possibly can about the operation. EDUCATION precedes DEDICATION. Include some personally interesting and uplifting courses for the workers to choose from. You want to convey the message that you care about the whole person. Show that you are interested in helping each one become a better person.

Here are some examples of programs and classes I believe employees would be interested in:

Marketing our product/
   service
Finish high school
Family planning
Financial planning
Physical fitness
Stress management
Positive thinking
Political awareness
Voter registration
Organization's history

Labor/management
   objectives
Alcohol and drug
   information
Child care and the
   working mother
Single parenting
Marriage enrichment
Handling teen-agers
Life after divorce
Outlook on aging

Company finance	Job re-training
All benefit plans for employees	Self improvement
	Art appreciation
Any kind of motivational courses	Travel opportunities
	"Stop smoking" classes

I am sure the enlightened management team will be able to "read" its employees and find interesting subjects to study and explore. This will cost very little and be very beneficial to both labor and management and will say to the workers, WE CARE ABOUT THE TOTAL PERSON.

The Office Staff
Must Be 'People Oriented'

A frequent bottleneck in maintaining good employee relations is found in a lot of administrative offices where staff members deal with workers in regard to benefits, pay, vacations, etc. Management should instill a mood of friendly, courteous helpfulness in these offices. After all, they are there to serve the employee as well as the company.

When an employee walks into an administrative office for assistance, he needs to feel that the clerk there is on HIS side. This clerk has to be a saint, with the wisdom of Solomon and the patience of Job. It might even take the strength of Samson to lift the weight of misunderstanding on the employee's part.

A prime example might be in the office that handles your employee insurance program.

Most companies have a designated, well-known insurance clerk. This must be a "people oriented" individual who can make sure the employee knows exactly what his policy covers and what is doesn't. All management should be careful not to say things that lead employees to expect too much, too soon, in insurance benefits. I have seen an enormous amount of animosity generated in the work place on this subject and it is not necessary. Be honest, open and aboveboard; lay it out in plain English; tell it like it is.

Don't say, "You will get $100 a week if you are out sick." That isn't true; an employee gets nothing the first week and may not get anything at all until he is back at work. A lot of people I have worked with got sick and were looking for that insurance check the first Friday they did not get their regular pay check. When they didn't get it, they weren't mad at the insurance company, they were mad at their employer. Make sure that every employee knows exactly what he will get in the way of insurance and when.

Don't just say, "$150 deductible." That doesn't mean a thing to many workers.

Say instead, "If you get sick, you will have to pay the first $150 of your medical bill and you will have to pay $20 of every $100 after that. No insurance pays everything anymore, so don't get sick, or get a backup policy."

The clerk could explain that when insurance companies were paying all the bills, people took advantage of it—"They took vacations at the hospital and let the insurance pay for them. As usually happens, a few spoiled it for everybody. It's not just our company; all companies are covering less and charging more for it."

Say something like, "I'm sorry, but we just want to be sure all our people know what to expect so they can be prepared. We also want to help you and your family stay well any way we can, that's why we have a physical fitness program, nutrition information, a company nurse on duty to give flu shots, blood tests, etc."

So, impress on all staff members in the administrative office, especially the insurance clerk, that they should remember:

Make sure the employee knows you are on HIS side when he or his family needs help. YOU CARE!

Management And Labor Are On The Same Team

Supervisors, you should keep in mind that we all are on the same team. Bosses are on the management squad; workers are on the production squad; but it's the same team. It is not one against the other, but US—TOGETHER—against our opposition.

WE ARE ON THE SAME SIDE! Put this in our computers.

It is US against competition.

It is US against inflation.

It is US against excessive government regulation.

It is US against foreign imports.

It is US against anyone who would divide us or out-produce us. It is just like the law of the jungle, we are dependent on one another. In Kipling's Second Jungle Book, he wrote:

"Now this is the law of the jungle,
It's as old and as true as the sky,
And those who keep it shall prosper,
But those who break it must die.
As the creeper encircles the oak tree,
This law runneth forward or back,
And the strength of the pack is the wolf,
And the strength of the wolf is the pack."

We are totally dependent on one another; if it were not for the expertise of management, Labor would have no jobs; if it weren't for the skills of employees, there would be nothing to manage.

There never should be an adversarial relationship between management and labor. We go forward together or we don't go forward at all. We should be friends, getting along well together, cooperating not only to close ranks against our foes, but to meet the demands of today's consumers, ever growing and reaching for new and higher goals, building a future for all of us.

When one considers the alternative, it is clear that labor and management must close any gap that exists between them.

Why? Because the only perfect man who ever set foot on this planet said, "If a house be divided against itself, that house shall not stand."

The buzz word for us is UNITY.

UNITY . . . YES!

"United we stand, and divided we fall"
It's a statement we often may hear.
When applied to the Labor/Management house,
The message today is quite clear.

For most of the programs and plans for the past,
That were used in employee relations
Have become obsolete in an enlightened era,
Of technology and education.

Those old outdated employment practices,
Where workers were prodded and pressed,
Produced adversarial relationships,
And nobody was doing their best.

NOW, the managers and managed are walking in step,
With allegiance and loyalty.
Proud and productive we are charting a course,
That decides what our future will be.

For success is elusive, never guaranteed.
To achieve it requires many things,
The greatest of which is THE WILL TO WIN,
That we get when we work as a team.

Yes, we're Labor and Management investing our skills,
Our energy and years of our lives.
We receive satisfaction and the mutual rewards
Of a prosperous enterprise.

As we settle our differences, and solve our disputes,
Our common good judgment will guide us
At all times presenting a united front
To those who may hope to divide us.

When we're shoulder to shoulder, we're the best we can be.
On this closeness our victory depends
For we must have a caring, cooperative spirit,
Or we may not be able to win.

Everyone is important, for we all have to make
Contributions uniquely our own
As we pool our resources we GO FOR THE GOAL,
That no one can reach all alone.

Yes, It's UNITED we move on to greater endeavors,
It's UNITED we grow and we build.
Only UNITY provides the competitive edge,
That can make us the best in our field.

So, we go forward together, or we don't go at all.
The choice is in our own hands.
UNITED . . . We're safe . . . But the alternative is . . .
A DIVIDED HOUSE . . . SHALL NOT STAND . . .

                                        Mark 3:25

                            Mildred Ramsey

Promote A Team Spirit

"Teamwork" is a word that management has batted around for decades, but the truth is that most employees in most industries do not see themselves as members of a team.

The cause is evasive, secretive, distant, insensitive "ivory tower" management.

Most of us just go in, do our jobs and watch for quitting time, never knowing or caring about how our particular part of the operation is connected with what employees in other departments are doing and how it all comes together in a finished product or service that we must sell in the market place.

A "team spirit" is being touted and talked about in management circles today. I hope it is becoming a reality in work places all over this country.

Everybody likes to be a member of a team. I had a boss once who had the right ideas for promoting a team spirit. His first night on the job, he called us to a meeting. As we all sat there looking him over, he said:

"My name is Buck Smith and I am your new supervisor. I thought we would talk just a minute or two and get acquainted.

"I know that every one of you is human and all have a certain amount of goofing off you're going to do. All I ask is that you keep it to a minimum. I'm human, too, and you may see me goof off sometime, but I promise to keep it to a minimum also.

"I also know there will be times when you can't come to work. If I don't have anybody to do your job, that's just my hard luck. All I ask is that you don't stay out unless you have to. We all have chosen this plant to work in and earn our living. It is to our mutual benefit if we do a good job and keep our company strong and competitive.

"You all understand, of course, that I have to require you to run the job you are being paid to run, but I don't want anybody killing himself here. If you feel you have too much to do, come to me and I will check it out."

Then he said something none of us will forget.

"Now, I know you are not going to be satisfied with ME 100 percent of the time," (He didn't say he wouldn't be satisfied with US.) "But, you are not satisfied with your husband or wife 100 percent of the time."

(Some of us weren't satisfied 50 percent of the time!) This super supervisor kept on:

"We spend one third of our lives together on this job. We spend more time with our work family than we do our real one, if we don't count the time we sleep. That's a big chunk of our lives, too much to be fretting and fussing. I want us to work together as a team; every member cooperating with the others to achieve top job performance—something we can be proud of.

"If I drop the ball, I hope you will recover it; if you drop it, I promise I'll grab it."

And, last of all, he addressed the problems of a team:

"We all know that no matter how hard we try there are going to be some problems among us from time to time. I just want to say that whenever trouble arises, if it concerns you, I promise to give you the benefit of any doubt. All I ask is that you do the same for me."

When we walked back to work, he had us all in the palm of his hand, and we had very few problems on that job.

He took a simple, common sense approach. He told us what he stood for and what he wouldn't stand for; he told us what was in it for us. He made us feel like a team; he gave us the game plan.

He was enthusiastic – always. Enthusiasm is the indispensable ingredient for a successful team. Remember, Supervisors, enthusiasm is not taught – it is caught! (Repeat that now and then as I do.)

What is the score?

Are we winning or losing?

How far ahead are we?
What is the strategy?
What are our long-range goals?
Short-range goals?
A good team manager doesn't keep his players in the dark.

Don't Discriminate

I once made a speech to a group of engineers in a city where my pro-freedom activities were well known. The first man I saw told me in a belligerent tone:

"I want you to know that my mother has been a member of the union for 40 years," he said, and proceeded to tell his story:

"My mother worked in a plant where they had what they called 'spare hands.' [These were extra people who might or might not get to work on a given day.] She noticed that each boss would face a group and point out the workers he wanted that day and they always overlooked her and chose the pretty ones. But, she got even with them. She joined the union."

I didn't get to talk any more with my bitter acquaintance, but I could not forget what he said. Here was a woman who paid union dues for 40 years, not because she liked the union, but because she was discriminated against because of her appearance. Her son was still mad about it, declaring that she "got even" with her bosses.

Talk about a lasting antagonism! Now, I don't know how ugly his mother was; she may have lost a beauty contest with an oyster, but the message here is plain—Mr. Supervisor, do not favor one employee over another, especially because of looks.

Don't discriminate against an employee who is fat—I don't care if elephants throw peanuts at her when she goes to the circus, you show her the same consideration you show your slim workers. One may be able to take a shower without getting her feet wet, but remember again, all employees have feelings and a degree of intelligence and you must treat them all the same. If you find it hard to do, keep in mind, this is part of your job.

The educationally disadvantaged worker must be treated

the way you treat a college graduate; the alcoholic the same as the total abstainer; the promiscuous woman as the deacon's wife; the black and white alike; etc. Everybody is somebody on your job because everybody is equal to everybody else.

This is one of the things we mean when we say we want to be treated "right," like a human being. We want to be treated equally and, Mr. Manager, you will forget this at your own peril. This is where we judge you on "fairness."

If your employees can say truthfully that you treat every one of them exactly alike and that you use the same tone of voice to everybody on the job day in and day out, you are a sensitive supervisor and my hat is off to you. If this is not the case, clean up your act before somebody decides to pay union dues 40 years to get even with you.

We are all equal—we are just in different roles.

Don't Surprise Employees

Management will create a lot of criticism and discontent by making changes in work procedures without advising employees in advance of what they are and why they are being made.

Even slight changes without explanation may upset your workers. An example of this occurred once when management decided to add only one loom to each weaver's job. It was considered "stretching out the weavers"—more work for the same pay. A friend told me the change went into effect at midnight Sunday—with no previous notice—and angered the workers.

"Right now, the whole weave room is anti-management," she said.

It was not so much what management did; it was the way it was done. It would have taken just a little time for the boss to call the weavers aside on Friday and say something like this:

"This is what we are planning to do and this is why. If it doesn't work, we'll try something else. I just didn't want you to come to work next week and find a change you didn't know about. If you have any problems with the new arrangement, we will work them out together."

Don't surprise employees with job changes, boss switching, policy changes, etc. Tell them in advance. This says to the workers, you are important, your confidence is needed, your feelings are being considered, your rights are being protected, your intelligence is being respected, you are valuable members of this team.

Don't let them find out from the bulletin board—YOU tell them. Ninety-nine percent of working people will go along with changes, even if they mean more work or less pay, IF management has the courtesy to explain the reasons and get employee input before the fact. This is a good way to make employees feel they BELONG!!!

Settle Employee Grievances Quickly

A "reformed" union organizer spoke recently at a personnel association meeting. He told these management people the best thing they could do to keep the trust and confidence of their workers was to have a good, fair grievance procedure.

A good grievance procedure recognizes the employee's right to disagree with you. We are not robots, we are human beings. We want to tell you what is bothering us on the job —and we want you to listen. Furthermore, we want you to do something about our complaints right away.

I called a friend in a plant where the union is recognized and asked what the union is doing for its members there.

"Nothing as far as pay raises and benefits are concerned," he said, "but they are getting grievances settled. If somebody has a problem and management won't do anything about it, he calls the union hall and it is settled in 24 hours."

Mr. Manager, if a union can make you settle a grievance in 24 hours, you ought to be able to do it without being forced.

You should have a "24-hour club" or something like that.

It will not be the big things that cause trouble, but the little things.

One time a couple on a safari got lost in the jungle and didn't show up until a day later. Their friends were happy to see they had survived such a dangerous experience.

"You must have been scared to death of all the alligators, lions and tigers," one said.

"No. We never saw an alligator, a lion or a tiger, but the gnats and mosquitoes almost ate us up," they answered.

It is the little things that eat you up on the job. You need a "gnat" and "mosquito" man.

Grievances generally fall into two categories: frivolous and serious. A suggestion box will take care of the frivolous ones nine times out of ten. Call it a "gripe box" or label it "complaints" and let a committee of employees (and maybe one management person) open it once a week – and let your people solve their own problems.

An important fact that lots of management people forget when they refuse to have a suggestion box is that it has value as an "escape valve." Once a complaint is written on a piece of paper, it is half solved. Especially the gnat and mosquito variety. So, have a suggestion box in every department.

Serious grievances should be taken at full value, Mr. Supervisor. Don't use that "I'll get back to you later" stuff. If you have to delay a decision, say something like, "I will try to get some action as soon as possible. Just in case I fail to give you an answer in a few days, YOU get back with me on it again – say by Friday."

Friday is not now – but it is definite. An employee will give you some time on a complaint if you show him you really want to do what is right. By Friday, he may have forgotten all about it. But, just in case, be prepared to settle it FRIDAY.

Problems ignored, neglected or put on "hold" do not go away. They settle like silt in an employee's mind. This is a time bomb! Address your workers' grievances as they arise. Try your best to settle them to the satisfaction of the employee – and do it fast.

If you don't – remember, thousands of companies have been organized by unions because of the lack of a good grievance procedure and, at the least, these unconcerned supervisors may be like Wong's employers. They may not know it, but they probably are drinking a lot of contaminated coffee.

Discipline—Correct
Without Condemning

A lot of good supervisors have shortcomings in the area of discipline.

Once in my early years as a weaver, I was moved to a new department. My boss came up one morning and said he was glad to have me on his job and appreciated my work, adding, "Your reputation as a dependable worker is well known."

"But, Mildred," he continued, "You are talking a little bit too much on the job."

There aren't too many ways to tell a woman she is talking too much, but I didn't get angry with him. Why? Because he gave me a good report before he gave me the bad one. This is the key to correcting someone without condemning them. You want to help without humiliating.

A supervisor's positive communication can inspire, excite and stimulate, even in a reprimand. If an employee has made an error, a positive approach would be, "This error is not a sample of your usual good work. Tell me what hindered you."

Non-condemning statements open up a dialogue and provide grounds for working out problems. Rehearse the discipline interview in your mind before you approach employees.

Remember this, too—always have your facts before taking a disciplinary action. Don't blame a person for something somebody else did. We hate this in a boss. Remember also, Mr. Supervisor, when you are wrong, admit it.

I never will forget a boss who came to me one day and referred to a bad roll of cloth he had been upset about the day before and for which he had blamed me. He made a simple apology, telling me he had learned the cloth was from another weaver's loom.

"I should have had my facts straight before I said

anything to you," he said. "I want you to know I'm sorry for blaming you for somebody else's mistake."

That boss never looked better to me than at that moment. He looked 10 feet tall.

Anytime a supervisor can go to a subordinate and say, "Hey, look, I was wrong, I'm sorry, I apologize, forgive me," that superior is cementing a solid relationship with the subordinate and his status as management material rises like a skyrocket.

So, Mr. Supervisor, when you are wrong, admit it. Everybody will try harder for this kind of boss.

A similar incident comes to mind from a time when I had a different supervisor. I found that he had been wrong about a roll of cloth he erroneously charged to me and told him so, adding that I had not had "any defects, or seconds at all yesterday."

"Well, that don't make any difference, you'll probably have some tomorrow," he said.

Which was true, but not to the point. He wasn't man enough to admit he had been wrong and I had no desire to please him the next day, or any time.

Supervisors, sometimes in daily contacts with your people you are going to be wrong. Parents, spouses, teachers, friends, all of us, sometimes are going to be wrong in personal relationships. When you are, admit it—this is a real motivator.

Anytime a supervisor goes to an employee and says, "I was wrong," he shows he is made of human stuff and he will endear himself to that subordinate and I guarantee the employee's "want to" will be stimulated in a very special way.

Another point to remember when administering discipline: Don't use sarcasm, exaggeration or unfounded statements in communicating with employees.

I once knew a boss who was inclined to overemphasize his points with sarcasm and exaggeration. One day he was upset about low job performance and told a worker, "My 12-year-old son could run this job better than you can."

A little later, I saw this woman come in the restroom and get her coat and asked where she was going.

"Home," she replied.

"Who's going to run your job?" I asked.

"Let him get his 12-year-old son to run it," she said, and away she went.

This remark by the supervisor not only was sarcastic and an exaggeration, it was a thoughtless lie, obviously meant to belittle the employee and shame her into better work habits. This type of communication does not motivate and inspire anyone to do better work. It backfired in that case and it will every time. Not every employee will walk out on you physically, but most will walk out mentally and emotionally and the job will suffer one way or another.

I know most management teams have been trained toward more positive techniques, but in case you ever are tempted to "jump on" an employee in this manner, don't do it. Only a super dumb person could imagine that infuriating someone, embarrassing and insulting him, will produce good results.

The problem in this particular case was that this boss was not management material. He was a "toe" and his people hated his guts and his ugly, angry and negative attitude toward them wound up hurting him more than it did those he vented it on.

This boss died of a heart attack a few years later, still a young man. He never got his people's best efforts.

Don't ever yield to the urge to use sarcasm, exaggeration or careless false statements on anyone you are trying to motivate. You will turn them "off' and they will close their heart's door tight against you—and they will mess up your coffee at the very first opportunity.

Temper Discipline With Mercy And Common Sense

When you administer discipline, you don't want to break your employee's spirit, bruise his ego and lower his morale – or create a lasting antagonism.

I know there are times when employee logic can be baffling – like the lady who came back from lunch an hour late and was asked by the boss why she was late.

"I got my hair cut," she explained.

"You can't get your hair cut on company time," the boss said.

"Well, it grew on company time," she retorted.

Another worker went to sleep on the job, grounds for termination in most organizations. He was leaning on his machine, his head resting on his arm so nobody could see he was dozing. After a while, he opened his eyes, still looking down, and saw his boss' feet. A fast thinker, he raised one hand and said, "In Jesus' name I pray, Amen."

That boss may have had strong doubts that the fellow was praying, but it always is a good idea to give an employee the benefit of the doubt when possible. He will repay you in performance and the day might come when you want HIM to give YOU the benefit of a doubt.

Too many organizations have the slogan: To err is human – to forgive is not company policy.

You can run a tight ship and rule your people with an iron hand, IF you put a soft glove on it. This is all employees ask. We know you have to do your job; we know you have to "get on" us at times; we know you have to correct us and instruct us. It is not what you do that turns us off or causes us to mess up your coffee – it is the way you do it.

The Super Supervisor uses courtesy lavishly in his employee communications. He thinks the discipline interview through before he has it. He speaks slowly and thoughtfully. (When people talk too fast, they are apt to say things they haven't thought of yet.) He never talks to an employee when he is angry. He never loses his temper at work. (When you lose your temper, you lose your case.) He is careful not to lose his associates' respect and support.

We need each other's support.

There's a story about two boys who bet a third youth they could walk 100 yards on a railroad track, one on one rail and one on the other, without falling off. The third boy took the bet because it is virtually impossible to stay on a track that far.

Well, the two boys stepped onto the rails and joined hands for balance. They had no trouble walking 100 yards supporting each other.

The Super Supervisor knows that when we don't support each other in the work place, everybody suffers – we can't stay on track.

One good way to keep the support of your employees is to temper your discipline with mercy and common sense and try to give them the benefit of any doubt.

When It's Time To 'Get Tough'

The words "getting tough" are batted around a lot among management people.

No. 1 Boss may say to No. 2 Boss, "It's time to get tough with Joe Doe," or he might say, "Maybe a little getting tough with a few employees would improve efficiency in your department."

By "getting tough," they mean verbal abuse in the form of veiled threats, demeaning, belittling remarks and other "put downs" of employees having problems. Most management teams agree that there are times when they have to "get tough" through insistence on following procedures more closely, strict adherence to policies, and elimination of lackadaisical performance or attitudes. They don't all agree, or admit, that there wouldn't be nearly as many of these "times" if sensitive supervising was in place "all the time" in all levels of management.

Let's take a hypothetical case from the employee's perspective:

An employee is not doing his job. As his boss, it is your job to find out why and correct the situation. You feel it is time to "get tough."

1. Go to the employee one-on-one.
2. Maintain a gracious, non-condeming tone of voice and manner.
3. Give him the facts.

"Tom, such and such has happened on your job. I double checked to make sure the error was yours. (Be sure you did double check.) This type of thing is not your normal pattern, so I know there must have been some reason for this mistake. Maybe you haven't been feeling well, maybe you have problems at home, or maybe you think I'm not doing my job right. (A good boss will take more than his share of the blame and less than his share of credit.)

"If there's anything you want to talk to me about, that's what I'm here for. You know I have to require every employee to do the job he is paid to do, but I don't want to be unreasonable and your feelings are important to me because we all have to feel good about ourselves and the job so we can do our best. (Good will equals good wares.) Now, how about telling me what is bothering you?

"Let's work it out so you can get back to your usual good work."

I can tell you, as an employee, that this style of "getting tough" will get management what it wants from workers a lot quicker than the old way of browbeating and pressuring. It will make a difference between RESPONSE and REACTION to your efforts to communicate.

There isn't one employee in 1,000 who won't respond favorably to a sensitive, sympathetic supervisor. Mr. Manager, why not try this "new" way of "getting tough" next time?"

It is called positive communication.

Positive Communication Gets Response Negative Communication Gets Reaction

Be Fair To Employees In A Dispute

A plant manager told me about a recent controversy in one of his departments where an employee and the first-line supervisor were at odds over whether the worker had made a proper report when out sick. The employee said he did, the supervisor said he didn't. Since this report would determine whether the worker would receive holiday pay, it was not solely a matter of who was right and wrong. Money was involved.

"I assume you are going to give the employee the benefit of the doubt, aren't you?" I asked the manager.

"Yes," he said, "but you must remember that I also have a responsibility to my first-line supervisor, so I'll have to handle the matter so the employee gets his pay and there is no lasting damage done to the employee/supervisor relationship."

"What will you do?"

"I'm meeting this employee tonight and I'll ask him to get a statement from his doctor that he was sick on the day in question. This is a long-established company policy on sick leave during a holiday period, so it is a reasonable request. I'll ask George to bring his statement to his supervisor and then he will receive his holiday pay – and the supervisor will not lose any stature in George's eyes because of the misunderstanding."

This was a great way to settle a disagreement to everybody's satisfaction when it is referred to upline management. Always try to give the employee the benefit of the doubt, especially if money is involved.

Of course, management is not looking for ways to beat workers out of money that is rightfully theirs, but sometimes the two views of what is right and fair differ.

I believe the wise management team will avoid any action that could make an employee feel he is being "cheated" in any way, especially financially. Give him the benefit of the doubt and some day he may do the same for you.

Don't Take Sides In Employee Disagreements

Every first line supervisor will at various times be drawn into an argument between workers. If you take "sides" with one against the other, you may damage your credibility as a leader. A good boss can settle a dispute between subordinates without alienating either side.

The pastor of a church I once attended had a fair and simple rule that put him above the role of "referee" among his flock. It worked beautifully for him and eliminated most bickering and fault finding among the membership. The same principle, I believe, will work in any supervisor/subordinate situation.

This preacher stuck to a simple rule: "Don't anybody call me on the phone to make a bad report about one of my members, because I won't listen. If you have something to say about somebody in my church, bring that person to my home or office and we will sit down together and talk. Only if everyone concerned is present will I hear you on any controversy involving my people."

Don't let one employee talk to you about another unless both are present. Make this a hard and fast rule, with no exceptions, and you will cut out most of the fussing and fighting among employees on the job.

Employees will respect and appreciate a boss who strives to prevent gossip and bad feelings among his workers. You can't be drawn into an argument if you refuse to listen to the details from only one side.

Diplomacy in handling your people problems will create harmony on the job and keep sand out of the gear box.

If You Make Changes—
Stick With Them

Employees are not stupid. If you need to make adjustments in your management policies, do it NOW.

A company vice president called me to ask if I could come to his plant and talk to employees about the advantages of working in a non-union shop. I asked if his labor lawyer would clear it and added, "You're not in an organizing campaign are you?"

"No," he said, "And it already has been cleared."

I went and it surely was one of the most emotionally rewarding speeches I ever made. I told the management team and about 75 workers some of my personal experiences and listed all the advantages I could think of in working together. I told the workers what they owed management and I told management what it owed its employees.

I never will forget it—nobody moved an eyelid for an hour. I knew I had accomplished something (a feeling I don't have every time). A few months went by and a man spoke to me in a store.

"I remember you," he said. "You spoke to us about labor/management relations. We were having a union "scare" at the time and for a while everything was different. We were having meetings with management and our employees thought it was terrific. But now . . ." he paused and shrugged his shoulders, "We are right back where we were."

I was astounded. I was so sure I had done some good. Later on, I called the vice president and told him what the employee had said.

"I'm guilty," he said. "What the man said is true."

"Why? Every one of those men, with one exception, was on my wave length. It's obvious you have a bunch of wonderful, loyal employees. Why did you change your techniques when the union scare was over?"

"Well, it just took up too much of my time."

I didn't ask any more, but I thought, "How much time do you think it might take to arbitrate, mediate, deliberate and negotiate a union contract?"

When a management team adjusts its policies during a "scare" and changes back to the old ways after it subsides, that management team is giving some malcontent the bullets to shoot it with.

Make Safety A Big Issue

Involve all your employees in the safety program. Most employers are fairly diligent in this area and, although no work place will be without a spot of oil on the floor, try to get workers to share with you that key word (again) "concern."

Show your workers you really do care about providing a safe work place, that you are trying to do so and that you are willing to listen to all safety suggestions. Urge employees regularly to report unsafe conditions and handle their reports immediately.

Management naturally does not want employees exposed to anything harmful, but sometimes is careless and slow about investigating and eliminating certain types of hazards, especially the "little" things. An antagonistic employee can take a puddle of water on the floor no bigger than a pancake and literally make a federal case out of it. It could cost you a thousand times more than it would to take measures to prevent it.

An unfriendly source (or bureaucrat) can make you appear to be the worst kind of rogue employer because you overlook some small safety hazard that might be a threat to employees, so keep your safety committees on the ball, active and excited about contributing to job safety. Work with them, convince them you're "concerned" and committed to safety.

And also remember—BE concerned. Employees know if you're faking or when your degree of concern is superficial.

Have A Fair And Simple Policy On 'Down Time'

"Down time" is a buzz word for the problem employee. He will walk about and exaggerate the small losses to workers because machinery is not working for some reason in a production operation.

Whatever policy you have, make sure those workers affected by it know exactly what it is. It would be great if these employees could have some input in formulating your "down time" policy, or maybe in reviewing and revising it. this certainly would be fair in the eyes of your production workers and they would understand why, in some circumstances, the company would "pay" and in some it wouldn't.

Ignorance of company policy among workers is the worst enemy of some supervisors. Educate your people on all company policies and procedures and you will wipe out one major pocket of discontent in your organization.

Don't Neglect Your Older Employees

For years, industry has had the reputation of using people up and throwing them away. You must convince your workers that you do not discriminate among them because of age or length of service.

Each one of your employees hopes to be old someday. I am not referring to material or financial matters concerning older people, but the attitude of supervisors toward this group is very important. Too often, when a person nears retirement age, he or she is overlooked, pushed aside and sometimes pushed out altogether.

A kind, courteous and compassionate relationship with the older group not only will get better job performance from them, but your younger workers will see your gracious concern and will respect you for it. They will feel secure about their own futures and do a better job also.

The wise supervisor will treat all employees alike anyway, so he certainly should not show less concern for the older ones. The employee who is 64 years old should be treated exactly like the one who is 19.

Do An Employee A Favor
If You Can

I once worked with a young woman you probably would call a "background" person on the job. She was not blessed with many attributes of appearance or social graces. She had a hard time financially and occasionally she would ask for her paycheck Thursday morning. We worked the shift from midnight to 8 a.m. and got paid Friday morning. In an emergency, the boss might give you your check Thursday. (Everybody knew checks came to the office each Wednesday.)

Well, the first line supervisor didn't want to give this girl her check on Thursdays because he did not like her, so he would make her wait. She would be tired from working all night and would stand in the hall, dozing. He would make her wait an hour or more sometimes and she hated his guts. (We did too.) If he intended to give her the check, he should have done it in private before stopping time; if he didn't, he should have told her he couldn't and make sure she understood why.

We are not idiots. If you tell us funds to cover payrolls are not deposited early, we will not ask again until the regular time. If there is no good reason to refuse, go ahead and give out a check to anyone who asks.

Do your employees a favor if you can. It will make them feel good about you and they will "want to" please you.

Supervisors, sympathy and compassion are two of the greatest motivators in the world. They should have taught you THAT in bossing school.

"Do unto others . . ."

Be A Peacemaker On The Job

Put out those fires in your work place. "Harmony oils the wheels of industry—friction puts sand in the gear box," is one way we have had it explained to us.

Most of my work life has been spent as a weaver in the textile industry. Weavers get paid by production and loom fixers have a lot to do with how much production a weaver gets in a given day—in short, how much money he or she makes. It is not unusual for a weaver to be hostile toward a fixer who stops off looms too long at a time. I have seen extreme cases where the entire weave room was affected. One weaver told me once that she had put two loom fixers in the insane asylum because of her never-ending pressuring and nagging about production. I wasn't that bad, but I remember one night my fixer stopped off two looms—I thought unnecessarily. I fretted and fumed and finally went to the boss.

"I'm so mad at Lee I could die. I just don't think I can work with that horrible man anymore," I told the supervisor.

"Why, Mildred," said the boss, "Lee thinks the world of you."

I said, "What?"

"Yeah, Lee loves to work with you. I heard him say the other night that you're one of the best weavers he ever worked with. He said he might as well take his tools when you flag a loom."

The boss put my fire right out. I looked at Lee and he didn't look nearly as bad as before. He liked me! He thought I was a good weaver. Well, I decided to show him just how good I could be and we never had any more trouble.

That supervisor was a peacemaker.

There is no way of knowing how long it had been since the boss had heard Lee pay me a compliment, probably months, but he saved it until he needed it. Always remember all the good things one worker says about another – the time will come when you can use them.

Everybody needs to feel good about their co-workers. Be careful when employees are angry at one another and don't add fuel to the fire like one other boss I had. I went to him one night and complained about another employee and he said, "I know it, he ain't no account. I would run him off if I could."

He poured gas on my fire.

Be a peacemaker. Many times the worst job situation in the world is not when people are upset with management, but they are angry with one another. No good work is going to get done in an atmosphere of disharmony and friction. The super supervisor knows this and always is on the lookout for ways to make his employees feel their common good outweighs any petty differences.

Remember, that was a wise person who said, "Harmony oils the wheels of industry – friction puts sand in the gear box."

Mr. Supervisor, be a peacemaker. It pays!

Use Extraordinary Concern
In Extraordinary Circumstances

A shuttle flew out of a loom one night and hit me on the head. (That's one of the things wrong with me.) A co-worker went with me to the rest room, then ran back to get my boss. He told her to come back and stay with me until he got somebody to go on my job.

No, no, Mr. Supervisor—you and I are friends; you care about me; we have a special relationship of mutual regard and if I get hurt, I don't want a co-worker with me, I don't want the department head, not even the plant manager—I want YOU, Mr. First-line Supervisor, and I want you right away.

You let somebody else take care of the work—you come running when an employee is hurt. Here is a beautiful example of what I mean:

One night at work many years go, I developed a strep throat and very soon was ill on the rest room floor. The second-level boss and the first-line supervisor came into the ladies room, picked me up and carried me to the car. The big boss said I was too sick to just go home and told me he was taking me directly to the hospital.

"But, I don't have any money," I told him.

"I don't care, you have to have some help, and the sooner the better," was all he answered.

The three of us sat in the emergency room a long time and several hours passed before I was treated. Now, here were both bosses off the job in the middle of the night for about four hours, but not one word was said about that by either of them. Neither said, "We better get back," or made any moves to rush my treatment—their only concern was that I should get the help I needed. They were kind and sympathetic as they took me home and I never forgot it. I paid them back in spades—

translated, performance.

This incident made me "want to" work harder than ever. I wanted to repay these super supervisors for their extraordinary concern in an extraordinary circumstance.

Supervisors, when an emergency occurs on the job involving one of your workers, drop everything and run to that person's side and stay until help arrives. This says, "You are important. I care about you."

This will motivate the socks off a subordinate.

One supervisor once drove his car right through a locked gate hauling an employee who had fainted and was turning blue. The gate was locked and nobody was at the gate house, so he just crashed through.

The employees all loved it.

That story went through the mill like prune juice—the supervisor cared about his employee and used extraordinary measures to help. Anybody going to work at that plant 30 years later would hear this story first thing. We never forget when you show you care.

Test yourself, Mr. Manager:

When an employee is injured or becomes ill on the job, in your first contact with him/her:

Is there warmth in your voice?

Is there compassion in your eyes?

Is there sympathy in your words?

Is there kindness in your attitude?

Is there understanding in your actions?

In other words:

Is your first concern for the best interest of the hurting employee, and,

Is your response exactly the same if the injured worker is NOT one of your favorites, or foreground people?

If you can answer yes to all these questions, I would say you are a super supervisor and are not having serious problems in this area of your labor/management relations.

Bless Yourself And Your Employees With The Light Touch

Save yourself and your people a lot of headaches, heartaches and ulcers by making use of the "light touch" in the shop.

Don't make "heavy weather" out of the little things that come up. It is said that a person's emotional health can be measured by the number of things he can "let go." So, let as many things go as possible when little problems arise.

Restroom gossip—let it go. Tattle tales—let them go. Rumors flying—let them go. Little rules, bent or broken—let it go. Don't waste valuable time and energy running down rumors and settling arguments—let them go.

If you refuse to give credence to, or get excited about, counter-productive nonsense on the job, your employees will follow your example. And they will quit bugging you about them.

So, relax. Don't take yourself so seriously. Don't come on strong to your employees. Use the light touch. A little good nature goes a long way in keeping the air clear and workers mentally alert and energetic. It is reported that good humor charges the body chemistry and increases creativity and I believe that's true. A light-hearted, relaxed person will get more work done in a shorter time.

As a boss, relax, smile, don't come on the job with a furrowed brow or drooping shoulders.

Enthusiasm is not taught—it is caught. A downbeat supervisor will have downbeat employees and will get downbeat work. On the other hand, "A merry heart doeth good like medicine," according to the proverb.

Be happy. Have a little fun at work when you have the opportunity. A cheerful nature and pleasant demeanor refreshes like a tonic. So, why not stay refreshed?

A word of caution: Don't have fun at an individual employee's expense. For instance, there was the case of the daily sheet listing each worker's name and certain figures about job performance and production. This sheet was given to supervisors at the beginning of each shift and they would discuss the statistics with each employee.

One worker's name was Whitfield. As you may know, the "S" on the typewriter is just below the "W" and one day the typist missed the "W" and hit the "S"—when the sheets were distributed, they didn't show Whitfield; it was another kind of . . . field. The supervisor showed the sheets around and pointed out the mistake, giving everybody a laugh. Everybody except Whitfield, who didn't think it was the least bit funny.

Supervisors must remember that it's to everybody's advantage to enjoy the light touch and to laugh with each other occasionally, but don't have fun at any one employee's expense.

Another interesting theory is that impossible goals may be reached with the use of the light touch. Don't tell your employees how to do a good job and enjoy their work—show them. Hang tough, but hang loose. Enthusiasm and good humor radiating from the boss will spread like wildfire over the job and that boss will find his people working harder and his own work will become easier.

The light touch—bless yourself with it; bless your employees with it; bless your world with it.

Managing people is a very stressful occupation and supervisors need to put the problems on the job in perspective.

I read an old Greek proverb that said, "You will break the bow if you keep it always bent."

Handling stress is a very important part of the supervisor's job. In my 42 years in textiles, there have been many times when an ambulance came to the plant to get a supervisor. It is not the hard work that burns you out, it is the stress involved.

We all need to take lessons from the ocean—it flows, then

it ebbs, then it flows, then it ebbs. Folks, we cannot flow all the time. If we don't ebb once in awhile, nature will do it for us. We will have a stroke, a heart attack, or accident.

When problems arise, we should give them the attention they are worth and no more.

I heard a preacher say one time, "Don't pay a Cadillac price for a Volkswagen."

This is good advice for all of us—especially supervisors.

Relax, the world is not going to explode if that project isn't done exactly on time.

Here is a quick way to relax—open your hands and turn them up. The tension will begin to leave you. Now, get your tongue in the middle of your mouth, not touching the top or lower jaw—you will feel relaxed immediately—Now close your eyes and let them roll back in your head. You can make yourself relax right there on the job. So, supervisor, go to your hiding place once in awhile (don't go around with your hands out and eyes closed on the job—everybody will wonder what you have been smoking.) Slip away for a few minutes when things get hectic and force yourself to relax. Things will straighten out sooner or later and you will live longer.

So think about the "light touch."

Relax!

Respect

Management must earn employees' respect.

I must tell you that, as an employee, I will not give my best efforts to a supervisor I do not respect. There must be a degree of respect in any interpersonal relationship and the greater that degree is, the more satisfactory that relationship will be. A leader must have INTEGRITY.

Respect must be earned. Here are some hints from employees.

Keep your hands off your people—no picking, poking, punching or pinching, patting or petting. The super supervisor has learned to communicate with his workers without handling them.

A handshake? Yes. A hug? No. You have to draw the line between friendliness and familiarity. You want to project an air of friendship, but be careful not to drift into a routine of familiarity with employees. Some employees may not see anything wrong in your patting and petting and a few might welcome it; but many will resent it and others watching are sure to misread your intentions, especially if you habitually touch your workers as you communicate.

"Handling" your people is demeaning, belittling. To most, when you pat them on the back, you are saying, "Good doggie, nice doggie." So, as you try to earn respect, "hands off!" Workers will respect you for this and work better with you.

Don't use profanity. Don't even say, "We're running a helluva good job." I will think more highly of you if you don't. As a supervisor, you are a cut above cussin' on the job. A profane person never can be a super supervisor.

Don't tell me any bad jokes. You can be jovial and friendly without them. Maybe no jokes at all on the job would be better.

Don't ask me personal questions. Of course, you can ask

about my children or where I went on vacation, but not about my "person." Don't ask where I bought my clothes or what kind of perfume I'm wearing or where I get my hair fixed. Personal questions are too close to familiarity and familiarity breeds contempt.

Don't tell me anything about your private affairs—or ask me about mine. If our relationship is one of friendship and trust, I may unload on you and cry on your shoulder sometimes and you should listen sympathetically, but don't give me any advice concerning my problems. I might take it and if it backfires, I will blame you. Just say something like, "Well, I hope you work this out because you are a good employee and I appreciate your confidence."

Always make your communication with your people "job related." You are emotionally interested IN me, but not emotionally involved WITH me.

Avoid any behavior at work that might have sexual overtones. Leave off questions ("How's your love life?"), insinuations, innuendoes, leering, standing too close, touching, whispering or gesturing. This is a no no for the upwardly mobile supervisor—he will keep his love life (or appearance of it) separate from his work life at all times. To be a cut above average, ACT the part.

The very worst thing a boss can do is become romatically involved with a worker in his company. There is no way this will work out for either party. First of all, it will be no secret. Mr. Supervisor, if you've got something going with someone in your organization, everybody there knows it. You could slip daybreak past a rooster quicker than you can get by with this. It is a silent motivation killer.

Nobody who works for you will walk up and say, "I know you are coming on to that employee in department X and you are not fit to be a boss and I am not going to give you my best work." But—they'll be thinking it and you won't get their best performance or respect.

This is not saying that all management personnel must be nuns or monks. Just keep your business life and personal life

112

separated. Your job, no matter what it is, is your business life. If you are a playboy or a playgirl, do your playing somewhere else. Take the advice given by an old grandfather to his grandson. He told the youth not to make a mess where he had to eat.

So, management personnel, the bottom line is: on the job, act like a lady or gentleman, whether you are or not and treat employees like ladies and gentlemen, whether they are or not.

Mutual respect on the job is very important, for when my respect for you goes, my "want to" do good work goes with it. Respectful behavior is part of the job.

Mr. Supervisor, you set the guidelines. You set the standards of behavior.

Employees need a stabilizing influence. They need to respect you. You must earn their respect every day by setting an example.

Remember, your reputation is made by many acts. It can be lost by ONE.

'Control'—The Word
For Supervisors

"Control" is the word for the supervisor, whether it is his temper, his tongue or his hormones.

In other words, Mr. Manager, if you want to supervise me, supervise yourself first.

You are a cut above average. You are supposed to be in control. Behave as if we all know it. A poet wrote about a pitcher named Bill Brown. Don't let his story be your story:

"Bill Brown had the speed of a thunderball,
He could loosen a brick from a 10-foot wall.
Everybody stood back when ole Bill let fly,
For no one could follow that ball's swift flight.
Now, Bill should have been playing in a major league role,
But ole Bill never made it 'cause he lacked control.
Now control is the thing, and there's no doubt about it,
And few ever get to the majors without it.
Now, you may have talent like the world's never seen,
It may even be greater than your wildest dreams,
And you may be wondering why the world won't extoll it,
But it never will happen 'till you learn to control it."

An air of adequacy and controlled authority will get you everywhere on the job. It will cause employees to "look up" to you and "want to" work for you. It never is too late, Mr. Supervisor, to work on your "control" in day-to-day encounters with your employees. If you have earned their respect, they will "want to" do a good job for you. Remember:

"The game isn't over 'till the very last inning,
And 'control' is the difference in losing and winning!"

If you want to supervise me—SUPERVISE YOURSELF FIRST.

Build Up Your Company
Or Organization

First line management never should be critical of the company when talking with employees. Supervisors should be looking constantly for ways to reinforce the workers' interest in and loyalty to the organization.

Mr. Supervisor, know only good things about our operation—and know a lot of them—as far as communication with your workers is concerned. When things are not going well with you and you feel "this place is the armpit of the world," don't relay this feeling to an employee.

Remember, first-line supervisor, YOU are the employee relations expert. You don't represent this company, you ARE this company to those working for you. What you tell us is what we will believe. So, "positive" is the word regarding our organization.

Don't "put down" upline management when you are talking to your subordinates. Employees need to feel secure about management. Your expertise is our foundation. Don't chip it out from under us by bad mouthing one another. We want to think our administrative personnel has it all together. After all, you are guiding our ship.

A mid-level boss never should make a derogatory remark about the chairman of the board in the presence of an employee—("John Doe is ruining this company," etc.) NEVER. If the board chairman is ruining the company, why should employees worry about job performance, loyalty, or anything else?

Bosses, you should reinforce your people's pride in your establishment every chance you get. The prouder an employee is of his company, the greater investment of energy he will make in it.

Program employee "computers" with lots of "positives" regarding our operation and its leaders.

As my supervisor, you don't know anything bad about our organization. Tell me the good things—how much money does our operation pump into the economy of this city every week? How many jobs have we created? How does my performance translate into job security! The Super Supervisor is "up," never "down."

Getting Rid Of Unproductive Employees Is Not The Answer

A supervisor may feel many times that getting rid of a trouble-making, negative-thinking, nerve-wracking employee is the solution to a problem. If you have one of these types who is resisting your efforts to motivate him to do a decent job, terminating him IS NOT the best remedy.

One time a group of social workers visited an insane asylum. They came upon a man pacing back and forth, back and forth, back and forth, his head bent down and saying, "Oh, Susie. Oh, Susie," in a mournful voice.

"What happend to that poor man?" asked one visitor.

"He had a sweetheart named Susie, but she deserted him and married another man and he couldn't handle it," was the reply.

The tour progressed and the visitors came to a padded cell where the occupant was tearing his clothes, pulling his hair, beating his chest and foaming at the mouth.

"What happened to this one?" the attendant was asked.

"He's the guy who married Susie."

You may get rid of a hostile and aggravating employee who is driving you crazy and get one in his place who will drive you crazier faster than the first one.

Somebody has to run that job and I don't care where you get an employee, where he comes from, or whose nephew he is, you are going to get a three-dimensional person. A worker cannot come into the work place and bring his body and leave his heart and mind in the car in the parking lot. The whole person comes and you are going to have to relate to all dimensions if you ever motivate him.

You might as well take the ones you already have, replacing them is not the answer. As someone suggested, "If you have a lemon . . . make lemonade.''

You really have no choice, Mr. Supervisor, you can't fire employees at will like you used to. The Super Supervisor will know how to get the best out of whatever he has—in other words—make lemonade.

In the next chapter, I will talk about how you can make this lemonade.

Motivating The Chronic Complainer

Sometimes when I am doing an in-house presentation, I have a question-and-answer period. Invariably, I get the question, "How can I motivate a chronic complainer?"—another way of asking, "How can I make lemonade out of my particular lemon?"

I got this question in Lexington, S.C., and I gave the supervisor who asked it my interpretation of that phrase:

Suppose your chronic complainer is a man whose son plays on the local high school football team. You read in the paper over the weekend that Lexington won. Monday morning you walk up to your employee, named Bill, who doesn't like you anymore than you like him. You would like to get rid of Bill, but can't; he is a thorn in your side; your relationship with him is anything but productive and you have decided to make a move. So, this day you approach Bill and say:

"Bill, I noticed in the paper that Lexington won the game Friday night. I know you are proud of that boy of yours, aren't you?"

You are applying the "AS IF" principle made famous by Norman Vincent Peale. You do not like Bill, but are going to act "as if" you do.

You know Bill is going to agree with you about his boy; he is going to smile and say, "Yes." You are having a POSITIVE ENCOUNTER with him. You planned it before you left home. (You have to plan these or they won't occur because most of us normally are negative in these situations.)

After you use the "AS IF" principle a few times, you may find you are not pretending, but have built on the little level of friendship you began with Bill—his attitude will change and the relationship will improve. As you plan other positive encounters with him, talking to him about things you know he will agree on, he will not be complaining so much—you have taken your lemon and made lemonade!

Plan POSITIVE ENCOUNTERS with people in your world and enrich those relationships.

Maybe your lemon does not have a son who plays football. Well, he has SOMETHING. What is his PASSION? What turns him ON? What winds his clock? Talk to these people about these things, plan positive encounters with them and you can make lemonade.

Supervisors, you need to know something about your people. What are their hobbies? What are their children's names? What is going on with these human beings outside the work place? Look at your employees and try to see some good in them. Everybody's beautiful in his own way. We all have good and bad points.

> My preacher says I'm a sinner,
> But my mother thinks I'm a saint;
> But both of them are mistaken,
> For neither of them I ain't.
> For a human being is a mixture
> From the moment of his birth,
> And part of me was made in Heaven
> And part of me was made on earth."

> Author unknown

I remember in school we learned a little verse:
> "There is so much good in the worst of us
> And so much bad in the best of us
> That it hardly behooves any of us
> To talk about the rest of us."

The secret is to look at someone and see the good and try to overlook the bad. Look at each individual's possibilities—not his limitations. See his assets, not his liabilities; his pluses, not his minuses.

Avoid negative encounters. Talk to people about things you AGREE on. Repair those ruptured relationships. Motivate those chronic complainers. Make lemonade!

The Impact Of Emotional Encounters

Experts tell us it takes what they call a "significant emotional encounter" in our lives to change attitudes, rearrange priorities or alter value systems. Remember the story about John?

John had a significant EMOTIONAL encounter when his boss asked about his mother and it settled in his mind forever what kind of work and how much work he would do for that boss.

It was a significant EMOTIONAL encounter for Merrill when he realized somebody did love him after all and it turned his life around.

I had a significant EMOTIONAL encounter when my plant manager came by and gave me some extra credit for extra effort I had put forth and it inspired me for 30 years.

It will be the POSITIVE emotional encounters with the people in your world that will mold and shape your relationship with them and enable you to STIMULATE, MOTIVATE AND ACTIVATE them.

POSITIVELY!

On the other hand, NEGATIVE emotional encounters will bring negative reactions. The relationship will suffer and neither party will give its best.

We are experiencing an emotional explosion in the work place today. The EMOTION factor must be dealt with positively.

I believe that the future belongs to the organization whose management team will grab onto this concept and ACTIVELY pursue a caring, sensitive and positive relationship with its employees.

Positive Emotional Encounters

Will

Inspire   **Encourage**

Influence   **Stimulate**

Motivate

and

Activate

Maybe Not 100 Percent

I know that some will not agree with everything in this book and make no claim to be talking about 100 percent of the people 100 percent of the time. There may be a weirdo in your world nobody can motivate, but I do believe that more than 98 percent of our population can be motivated by the principles I have emphasized.

As I said, there may be one or two exceptions. One time a swarm of bees was flying down a business street and all of them lit on a Texaco station—except one. He flew across the street and lit on an ESSO station. Now, the moral of this story is, there always is one Esso bee (SOB) in every crowd.

Why did that one little bee break away from the swarm? He just wanted some attention, didn't he?

Folks, remember that little bee the next time somebody "acts up" on your job, or in your world.

The Super Supervisor
Is Not Perfect

Your employees do not expect you to be perfect, Mr. Supervisor. We know that you are human and subject to having a bad day occasionally. However, if the Super Supervisor's normal pattern of behavior is kindness, concern, compassion and caring and if he is acting differently one day, his employees know that something is affecting him and they will give him their continuing support because they know what his normal behavior pattern is. They know this from past experience.

No, the Super Supervisor is not perfect, but he sees his people as persons first and employees second.

He recognizes his people's presence on the job every day, first thing.

He reinforces their positive behavior.

He recognizes their family priority.

He considers their feelings on the job every chance he gets.

He recognizes their ordinary ability and extra efforts on the job.

He recognizes their intelligence and utilizes it on the job.

He realizes that his employees' energy is forever bound up in their *emotions*, so he is careful in communicating with them.

He has EARNED his people's respect, their trust, their affection and admiration.

He corrects without condemning.

He influences and inspires his workers because he is neat, clean, confident and enthusiastic day in and day out.

His employees like him and "want to" work for him.

He gets top job performance out of his people on a continuing basis because he is a LEADER, not a PUSHER.

The Super Supervisor CARES about his workers; he makes them feel IMPORTANT because he thinks they ARE.

Management teams, I hope you have gotten the message—a good relationship with your employees will help you

INCREASE PRODUCTION
IMPROVE QUALITY
ENSURE LOYALTY

and help secure your operation's future.

The principles discussed in this book are simple, but they are sound. They are cost-free and, best of all, THEY WORK. They have worked on me hundreds of times; I have seen them work on my fellow employees thousands of times and they will work on your people.

I am closing with a poem I wrote several years ago titled "The Super Supervisor," which sums up what I have tried to say in this book. I wish you all good luck and God speed—and great coffee!

The 'Super' Supervisor

The "Super" Supervisor is the employee's friend,
He keeps discouragement out and encouragement in.
He works WITH his people and he wears a soft glove.
This boss doesn't push and he NEVER shoves!
By his smile and his manner, his employees will know
That he's reasonably content in his leadership role,
For he "handles" his people with concern and compassion
And his enthusiasm will NEVER be rationed.

INDIVIDUAL RECOGNITION is part of his plan,
And he praises his people when he sincerely can.
And a mutual understanding that is never depleted,
Makes employee discipline seldom wanted or needed.

Yes, the Super Supervisor balances the scale
Through his daily attention to each tiny detail.
And by working WITH people who give him their best
He has discovered the secret of a company's success.
No, it isn't new buildings, or a name on Wall Street,
Nor the elegant rooms where the board members meet,
It isn't the Rembrandt that hangs on the wall,
Nor the oriental carpet that graces the hall.
But a loyal and reasonably contented work force
Is ANY employer's most valuable resource.
So, the "Super" boss' people are not just subordinates,
Each one is RESPECTED and each one is IMPORTANT,
Each one is his EQUAL, just in a different role,
And TOP JOB PERFORMANCE is their mutual goal.

Yes, A "Super" Supervisor is the only essential
That keeps employees challenged to their highest potential.

Mildred Ramsey

NOTES

NOTES